The Q Guide to

The Golden Girls

The Q Guides

FROM ALYSON BOOKS

POP CULTURE

Q

OUT THERE

GUIDE

The Q Guide to

The Golden Girls

**Stuff You Didn't Even Know You Wanted
to Know** . . . about Dorothy, Rose,
Blanche, Sophia, and the beloved sitcom

[jim colucci]

© 2006 BY JIM COLUCCI

MANUFACTURED IN THE UNITED STATES OF AMERICA.

THIS TRADE PAPERBACK ORIGINAL IS PUBLISHED BY
ALYSON BOOKS
P.O. BOX 1253,
OLD CHELSEA STATION,
NEW YORK, NEW YORK 10113-1251

DISTRIBUTION IN THE UNITED KINGDOM BY
TURNAROUND PUBLISHER SERVICES
UNIT 3, OLYMPIA TRADING ESTATE
COBURG ROAD, WOOD GREEN
LONDON 722 6TZ ENGLAND.

FIRST EDITION: SEPTEMBER 2006

08 09 10 **a** 10 9 8 7 6 5 4 3

ISBN-10 1-55583-985-1
ISBN-13 978-1-55583-985-7

LIBRARY OF CONGRESS
CATALOGING-IN-PUBLICATION DATA IS ON FILE.

ILLUSTRATIONS BY GLENHANSON.COM
PAGE VIII PHOTOGRAPH COURTESY GETTY IMAGES

*To Bea Arthur, Rue McClanahan, Betty White,
and Estelle Getty—on behalf of gay people everywhere,
Thank You for Being a Friend.*

Contents

FROM LEFT TO RIGHT, DORIS BELACK AS GLORIA PETRILLO, ESTELLE GETTY, AND BEA ARTHUR IN "THE CUSTODY BATTLE" FROM SEASON ONE.

Foreword

BEA ARTHUR is ruining my love life.

It is a complaint I hear all the time. All over the country, domestic bliss is being shattered every day, because at least one partner in every couple I know is addicted to reruns of *The Golden Girls*. The classic sitcom airs so often on Lifetime—six times a day at last count—that the cable channel might as well tack three more words onto their slogan. "Television for women," we say aloud at every station break, "…and gay men."

The series is our favorite guilty pleasure. Day after day, and night after night, we tune in to hear Sophia turn the word "cannoli" into an Italian innuendo. We laugh at Rose's cockamamie stories—her grade school teacher back in St. Olaf, Minnesota, you'll recall, was actually Adolph Hitler in disguise—and we pity poor Dorothy for having to listen to them all. While we're at it, we take a few pointers from Blanche's man-hungry maneuvers, too.

We know all the jokes by now, but who cares? Despite their wardrobes, we love these old broads. But then the gay community always has. Whether we were hosting viewing parties at gay bars or dressing up as the girls for Halloween, *The Golden Girls* was a part of our lives, a shared reference point, and a common love. Can anyone hear the word "lanai" without thinking of those four seniors living and laughing together?

Why the show, which ceased production more than a decade ago, continues to be embraced by the gay community, however, is something I'm glad we're finally going to discuss here. After all, compared to more recent fare, it doesn't have the frank sexuality of *Queer as Folk*, the titillating nudity of *Oz*, or the party-hearty spirit of Karen and Jack on *Will & Grace*. But there is something special about *The Golden Girls* that gay men—and yes, some lesbians—adore. As Betty White once told me, "I don't know what it is with the gay community. I'm just glad it happened."

Here's my theory: *The Golden Girls* is about four roommates looking for love and not always finding it—except from each other. Men repeatedly ripped their hearts out—Dorothy's "yutz" of a husband Stan was always good for a few chest pains—but as long as there was a cheesecake in the freezer and three friends to share it with, each knew she'd survive. The show was *Sex and the City* with Maalox instead of martinis. Above all else, *The Golden Girls* was—and is—a paean to friendship.

Come to think of it, maybe we shouldn't feel so guilty about watching it.

—Frank DeCaro

Introduction

"PICTURE IT: August 24, 1984. Two actresses 'of a certain age,' each currently appearing on a hit NBC show, step out on stage at the network's Burbank headquarters. As presenters during NBC's Fall Preview special, they trade scripted patter from a teleprompter, and in the process, do more than a little ogling of a male lead in one of the peacock network's more promising new dramas. The object of their affection? None other than Mr. Don Johnson, then about to debut in the fashion—and decade—defining hit, *Miami Vice*. And the gawking gals, whose performance that night would inspire NBC president Brandon Tartikoff to commission a sitcom about the active lives and loves of the over-sixty set? They are, of course… Selma Diamond and Doris Roberts.

"What, you were expecting Bea Arthur or Betty White?"

And so might begin the story of *The Golden Girls*—well, at least the way Sophia Petrillo might tell it. And just like one of Sophia's trademark "Picture It–" stories, the tale of how one of the most beloved comedies of all time made its way to the small screen is not a straightforward one, nor is it very likely.

—*Jim Colucci, June 2006*

The Q Guide to
The Golden Girls

CHAPTER ONE

Getting Started

Q

QUOTE

"Brandon always came up with these wacky ideas, and some of them were genius and some were terrible. That's the sort of thing that happens with creative people who mine their inner child. You either get *Mr. Smith*, about the talking orangutan, or you get *The Golden Girls*."

–Garth Ancier, former head of current comedy at NBC

Miami Nice

IN TWENTY-FIRST century TV land, we may have more channels to choose from, but some things haven't really changed since 1985; then, as now, broadcast networks like NBC aimed their programming squarely at the advertiser-coveted 18–49 age demographic. So that night at the NBC presentation, when Selma Diamond, who was then appearing on the network's Thursday night sitcom *Night Court*, stopped eyeballing Don Johnson long enough to tell *Remington Steele*'s Doris Roberts excitedly that "there's this wonderful new show, all about retirees in Florida—it's called *Miami Nice*," it was obviously a joke—or was it?

In his 1992 memoir *The Last Great Ride*, the late former NBC chief Brandon Tartikoff remembers spending a rainy afternoon channel surfing with his seven-year-old niece, until they agreed on the 1953 Betty Grable-Lauren Bacall-Marilyn Monroe movie *How to Marry a Millionaire*. The straight, married Tartikoff was nonetheless struck by the idea: how about a frothy comedy about a group of women sharing an apartment together, waiting to meet Mister Right? There was just one problem: other people hated the idea, especially women. When he tried to recruit female writers to work on the project, they were offended by the idea of presenting the young, independent 1980s woman as being incomplete without a man. But the idea stuck in the back of Tartikoff's mind, and later, while visiting his elderly aunt in Florida and observing her crotchety interplay with her neighbor, he had another inspiration: make it *How to Marry a Millionaire for Women Over Fifty*.

"Brandon may not have shared those thoughts with us all, so I'm not sure how the *How to Marry a Millionaire* stuff ended up actually being connected to the development of *The Golden Girls*," explains Warren Littlefield, who was then the network's Vice President of Comedy Programs. But Littlefield does know that at what may have been the same time, the *Miami Nice* gag was gathering steam. "It had been the highlight of laughter in a long, boring shoot night," he remembers. "That Fall Preview special had all these hot young stars from other shows, but here were these two middle-aged actresses who stood up in the spotlight and *BAM*! They were sharp, they were hitting it, and they made their segment pop." A week later at Los Angeles's Century Plaza hotel for the network's off-site retreat, Littlefield, Tartikoff, and other executives tossed around ideas to develop into series for the 1985-86 season. As they recalled Diamond and Roberts's phenomenal performance, suddenly *Miami Nice*, the shtik about the ridiculousness of a "retirees in Florida" sitcom, didn't seem so ridiculous anymore.

From that meeting, Littlefield resolved to seriously develop *Miami Nice* as a sitcom for the following season. The timing was right to be daring; only one season after turning around its comedy fortunes with the 1984 debut of *The Cosby Show*, NBC had nowhere to go but up. And having succeeded by following gut instinct in airing *Miami Vice*—testing prior to the show's debut had predicted horrendous ratings—the

BEING A FRIEND: A CONVERSATION WITH DORIS ROBERTS

ONCE A YEAR, NBC would put on this big show to promote the fall lineup. I've always laughed because they'd have this great big peacock as the stage design, and to enter, all of the actors would have to come out through the ass of the peacock. I didn't ever quite understand what that was all about. But Selma Diamond and I had great fun with the *Miami Nice* bit. We had a script, but didn't have much time to rehearse, so we were sort of ad-libbing, too. Afterwards, Brandon said to us, "You girls are terrific together. I'm going to get someone to write for you."

I don't know what he said to Selma, but several months later, Brandon asked me to come to his office. He asked me, "Can you do two things at once?" And I said it depended on what he was thinking. He said, "We're going to have a script based on how you and Selma carried on that night. I can't let you go from *Remington Steele*, because you're too important on that, but it's up to you—do you think you can do them both?"

I told him I thought I could—after all, Nancy Walker once did two shows—but that wasn't the problem. I thought if the writers can't count on how much time they're going to have with you, they won't know how to write for you. They won't know what's important enough or

> what's big enough to give you to do in any given episode. And Brandon agreed with me. I didn't think it would be fair, and so I didn't pursue doing what later became *The Golden Girls*.

executives were ready to reach outside the 18–49 age group and defy convention one more time. "We felt like lightning had struck us with something," Warren explains. "We would look at those little charts in *USA Today*, and there would be some factoid like 'women over fifty have a one in eleven billion chance of remarrying.' It was always some sad statistic, and it reinforced what we were feeling about *Miami Nice*, that somehow, these women would be there for each other, and they would take a difficult reality and make a bright picture out of it."

Although Roberts and Diamond were already committed to other NBC series, the network knew they would have no problem casting a show about older women. "We learned a lesson in casting *The Cosby Show*," Warren remembers. "If we could have cloned Bill Cosby, then we could have created five more road companies of that show, because there was just so much talent from black actors who weren't being used on television. And the same thing happened with this show. There was a large pool of wonderful older actresses who weren't doing feature films and television, who were being ignored. And when we saw how similar that situation was to *Cosby*, we knew we were on the right track."

Q FACT: As the show was being developed, one of the alternate titles considered was "Ladies' Day"—which is ironic, considering the fact that *Miami Nice* muse Doris Roberts later used the phrase on her series *Everybody Loves Raymond* as a euphemism referring to a woman's period.

A Gay Among Girls

BEFORE RECRUITING a writer for the project, the network decided that *Miami Nice* would center on household life for several women, one of whom would own the house. At least one character would be older, to allow for intergenerational conflict. And there would be one more character, a gay houseboy.

Yes, in 1985—twelve years before Ellen DeGeneres's and her character Ellen Morgan's courageous coming out on ABC's sitcom *Ellen*, and thirteen years before NBC's own *Will & Grace*, the first series created specifically to have a gay leading man—a major broadcast network commissioned a pilot which was to feature a gay character. "Miami at that time was such a cool, happening place, and a gay character just felt like someone you might find in that environment," Warren explains. "To us, it didn't feel bold or outrageous, but organic. These ladies are probably not on their hands and knees, scrubbing. They've had a lot of years where they'd done all that stuff, so they would hire someone to help out. And we thought the gay houseboy would be a fresh character and a fun contrast to the women."

Only Hetero Love, Sidney

THAT ALL sounds logical—but as we all know, homophobia doesn't rely on logic, and networks don't always stand so tall against homophobia. In fact, just four years earlier at NBC, Tony Randall's Sidney Shorr was to have been network TV's first gay lead in the 1981–83 sitcom *Love, Sidney*, until internal network politics forced a change for the character. In the two-hour telemovie that launched the series, Sidney had been "not openly gay," explains the network's openly gay former Senior Vice President of Talent and Casting Joel Thurm. "But he was a lonely old man who had had a relationship with a man we see in a picture on his mantel, and at one point he goes with Laurie, the young single mother who with her daughter moves in with him, to an old Greta Garbo movie, so it's definitely implied."

When the *Love, Sidney* movie turned out to the development execs' liking, the future looked bright for a Sidney Shorr series. "But then," Joel remembers, "someone at the network, obviously a rabid homophobe who didn't want the project, slipped a copy of the movie to the network's sales department without authorization. And so the sales department came into program meetings and announced that because of the gay content, they couldn't and wouldn't sell it to advertisers as a series. And if the sales department is one hundred percent against a project, that's a very, very strong negative." Eventually, out of desperation as many of its other shows failed in the ratings, NBC did resuscitate *Love, Sidney* as a midseason replacement series—but not before turning gay Sidney Shorr into an asexual celibate. And that photo disappeared from the mantel, too.

Julie Poll, a television writer who worked as a production assistant on the series version, remembers NBC's Standards and Practices department—aka, The Censors—combing every word of *Love, Sidney*'s dialogue, eliminating any possible references to homosexuality. "I'll never forget, Laurie had a perfectly innocent line where she gratefully said to Sidney, who had taken her into his home, 'You're my fairy godmother.' But then the network saw it, and out it went." And she says, although both Swoosie Kurtz—who played Laurie in the series after the pilot movie's Lorna Patterson left to become CBS's *Private Benjamin*—and particularly Tony Randall continually fought to keep the original integrity of the characters, eventually, *Love, Sidney* became just another contrived sitcom (albeit one that featured future Golden Girl Betty White in a recurring role as an Agnes Nixon–like soap opera writer). "Originally there was a glue holding them together," Julie says. "Sidney adopted Laurie and her daughter as a family because he obviously wasn't going to have one of his own. Once he wasn't necessarily gay anymore, it didn't make as much sense. It had been a lovely, heartfelt friendship, and it was really interesting because it was something we hadn't seen before. And that's what changes television."

Enter Susan Harris

JUST A FEW years later, *Miami Nice*'s gay character might have suffered the same de-gayifying fate as Sidney Shorr; but, luckily for the houseboy, Littlefield got the idea through to writer Susan Harris, who had created one of TV's first gay characters, Billy Crystal's Jodie Dallas, on her first big hit comedy series, *Soap*. (Jodie may not have been *the* first regular gay character on American TV, but he was certainly the highest-profile to date, since few remember Vincent Schiavelli's Peter Panama on the short-lived 1972–74 CBS sitcom *The Corner Bar.*) But even the hiring of Harris happened by happy accident.

Paul Junger Witt and Tony Thomas—two-thirds of the then-growing TV powerhouse production company Witt-Thomas-Harris—had brought one of their writers in to present a new series idea about two young sisters living together to Warren Littlefield. Littlefield had been unmoved by the pitch, but, eager to steal away the producers of such hits as *Soap, Benson,* and *It's a Living* from rival ABC, he offered an idea of his own: how about you go off and develop *Miami Nice?* The writer—who is probably still kicking himself to this day—was uninterested. But just after seeing their scribe out of Littlefield's office, Witt and Thomas poked their heads back through the executive's doorway. "Were you serious about that idea?" they asked. Because Paul Witt had just the writer in mind.

Although she had sworn off writing for television

CELEBRITY SURVEY #1:

WHICH GOLDEN GIRL ARE YOU, AND WHY?

DOROTHY, because she was the most independent, worldly, and snappy of the roommates. She also was close with her mother, had a vulnerable side, and was the first to remarry, which is saying something. She was also the butchest and, let's face it, that's me!

—Billy Masters, syndicated columnist and performer

DOROTHY. I wear shoulder pads, I can kill you with a look, I'm the one with the loser exes, and I'm the one people go to for comfort, support and advice. Clearly it's not because of my height—I'm only 5'3".

—ANT, stand-up comedian and host of *VH1's Celebrity Fit Club*

DOROTHY. Same luck with ex-husbands.

—Doug Spearman, actor

BLANCHE, for the glamour (in her own mind), her reputation as a great lover (in her own mind), and all the other fabulousness she dreamed up.

—Ben Patrick Johnson, author of *Third and Heaven*

DOROTHY, because I think sarcasm is the greatest thing in the world, and if you don't "get it," then I'll freeze you out with my eyes. And, I do not suffer fools well.

—Tony Tripoli, actor,
My Network TV's *Fashion House*

DOROTHY, according to the quiz on the Lifetime website, which I'm totally okay with. Although I need to work on my withering glance.

—Dennis Hensley, "Twist" radio host and
author of *Misadventures in the (213)*

DOROTHY, because I'm tall and have been known to get in a good zinger.

—Bob Smith,
writer/stand-up comedian

SOPHIA. I wanted to grow up to have her candor. I practice being blunt in her honor now that I'm a mature man.

—Tom Bianchi,
artist/author

DOROTHY. She has the same kind of wit to her that I do, and also has a bit of an attitude problem—something I've been told that I do as well.

—Mark Lund,
television personality

DOROTHY, because she's the most levelheaded of the group.

-Keith Boykin, BET TV show host

DOROTHY. HELLO!?!?! Tall, sarcastic, GAY!!!

—Judy Gold, actress/writer/stand-up comedian

ROSE. Because she's a little naïve and constantly saying outrageous things rather inadvertently.

-Rex Lee, actor, HBO's *Entourage*

DOROTHY, because she had the quickest wit. But my friends say I'm more like Blanche because they think I'm slutty.

-Bruce Daniels, comic

DOROTHY, because of my disdain for ignorance. But I think all fags want to be Blanche, me included.

-Dan Mathews, vice president of People for the Ethical Treatment of Animals (PETA)

DOROTHY, obviously. Because she's tall, gray, and bitter. But I wish Blanche.

-Ted Casablanca, E! Online Gossip Guru and columnist of "The Awful Truth"

BLANCHE, duh. She taps right into my inner Southern Slut. Every gay New York Jew has got one.

-Dan Bucatinsky, actor/writer/producer

ROSE. She has a well-placed heart, but she's as naïve as you can get.

–Tammy Etheridge, actress/writer

DOROTHY, without a doubt. She's bossy and over-sensitive. I am not tall, however, and I may have been a little slutty Blanche years ago.

–Suzanne Westenhoefer, stand-up comedian and panelist, GSN's I've Got a Secret

SOPHIA, although I'm far too young. My radio co-host Romaine thinks I am Dorothy, but she is just saying that because I am so tall and dated a lot of losers. Can you believe that backstabbing slut?

–Derek Hartley, talk show host, Sirius Satellite Radio

ROSE, because of her honesty and innocence. Unfortunately, as I get older I feel more and more like Sophia every time I put on my reading glasses and squint to read the newspaper. It's only a matter of time before I buy a rhinestone chain to keep them on.

–Jaffe Cohen, stand-up comedian and author of the novel Tush

ROSE. Because I consider myself a hot-blooded Southern girl, I thought for years that I was a Blanche. But, alas, my friends have reminded me otherwise. Having spent time in Arkadelphia, Arkansas, where my parents grew up, and where my entire clan resides, I have a bizarre and often lengthy story for every occasion. Who can forget my true story about the man, Mr. Shannon, who lived next door to my aunt? He would dress up like a lady and run through my aunt's backyard. Then he would come over later, dressed as a man, and ask everyone if we had seen his friend "Bridget." The last I heard of Mr. Shannon was that when his wife died, he propped her up in his truck and drove her to Wisconsin, where she wanted to be buried. Have I gone on too long?

–Varla Jean Merman, cabaret performer and actress, *Girls Will Be Girls*

A combination of **BLANCHE** and **DOROTHY**. A li'l flirty, but with a lot to say.

–Randy Jones, original Village People Cowboy

My boyfriend thinks I'm **BLANCHE**, my coworkers think I'm **DOROTHY**, my business manager looks at me like I'm **ROSE**, and I think my son treats me like I'm **SOPHIA**.

–Douglas Carter Beane, playwright

A combination of **BLANCHE** and **SOPHIA**. An aggressive irritant.

–Jermaine Taylor, panelist, GSN's *I've Got a Secret*

A combination of **ROSE** and **BLANCHE**. A little dumb and a little slutty.

-John Bartlett, designer

I am equal parts **DOROTHY**, **BLANCHE**, **ROSE**, and **SOPHIA**—25% of each.

-Robert Verdi, stylist, actor, and host of Discovery Channel's *Surprise By Design*

There's a little bit of all of them in me, but I am most like **DOROTHY** because I am a man.

-Craig Chester, actor/writer/director of *Adam & Steve*

SOPHIA. She's an old Italian-American broad with no censoring mechanism and a killer red sauce recipe. But on stage, I'm really more like Count Bessie, the piano-playing chicken.

-Frank DeCaro, talk show host, Sirius Satellite Radio, and panelist on GSN's *I've Got a Secret*

After one cocktail, I'm **BLANCHE**. Isn't everyone?

-Bruce Vilanch, writer/performer

WHICH GOLDEN GIRL ARE YOU—AND WHY?

after burning out during the intense production of *Soap*, Witt's wife and producing partner Susan Harris was taken with the *Miami Nice* idea the moment her husband came home with it. "As soon as he used the word *older*, that got me," Susan remembers. "I love to write old people, because I find that the older the character, the better the stories he or she has to tell. So that was the hook for me—that I could write about an interesting demographic that had really been ignored." Together, Witt, Thomas and Harris, who had been a creative entity since the days of their first series, the Lee Grant-starrer *Fay* for NBC in 1975, brainstormed the structure of the series: three women, a mother, and of course that gay houseboy. "When I felt comfortable there was enough stuff, we pitched the story to the network, and then I went off and wrote it," Susan says.

The Golden Girls

A FEW MONTHS later, Warren Littlefield received delivery of a Susan Harris script, now entitled *The Golden Girls*. The new title immediately started to grow on him—after all, the network had been wondering, how can we possibly risk confusing our audience by airing both *Miami Vice* and *Miami Nice*, two vastly different series whose titles differed by only one letter? But *Girls*? "I had a moment where I wondered, it's the '80s—can we call grown women girls?" Warren remembers. "I brought that up to Paul and Tony, and they said, 'Yes, Susan says we can say *Girls*.' And I said, 'Okay—if she says so.'" And so, in that newly retitled script which NBC read and immediately loved, four *Golden Girls* named Dorothy Zbornak, Blanche Devereaux, Rose Nylund, and Sophia Petrillo were born.

CHAPTER TWO

Meeting (All) the Girls

"In the beginning, Brandon Tartikoff and the people at NBC all thought, 'Let's not go the tried-and-true way and just give America a bunch of familiar faces. Let's go to Broadway and Chicago and cast some faces they don't know.' We thought that was odd, but we did then go out to those cities and see many, many women—and nobody was quite right. We could have done the whole process in three minutes otherwise. After all, the stars we ended up bringing in were stars for a reason. It was just luck that they were all available for a series."

–Tony Thomas

FOR ANY FAN of *The Golden Girls*, the name Dorothy Zbornak probably conjures up the image of a tall, imposing woman in a long, cowl-necked tunic. But how much do you truly know about the characters of Dorothy, Blanche, Rose, and Sophia? Two of the show's creators, Susan Harris and Paul Junger Witt, remember how these four quite different ladies sprang forth from the pilot's pages.

Dorothy Zbornak

RECENTLY DIVORCED from Stanley, her philandering husband of 38 years, brainy ex-Brooklynite Dorothy is a no-nonsense substitute schoolteacher who undoubtedly takes no prisoners in the classroom. "Dorothy was the easiest character for us to come up with," Susan explains, "because Paul and I are from the New York metropolitan area. And she had a mouth on her." And, Paul adds, "A sarcastic, cynical voice we could hear fairly early."

Susan says she may have been conscious of the name Dorothy in honor of either Paul's aunt or her own childhood friend. But the origin of the character's unusual last name is much more clear—she cribbed it from her assistant Kent Zbornak, who later became a producer on the show. "Zbornak is such a great, real-sounding name," Paul says, for a real, take-me-as-I-am character. (For the record, Kent says, the name is of Czech extraction.) "We are a nation of immigrants, and Zbornak sounds as American as Jones or Andersen or anything else." Not to mention—it just sounds funny.

Rose Nylund

A **WIDOW** originally from the apparently wholly moronic town of St. Olaf, Minnesota, naïve Rose somehow finds the wisdom to counsel others at a grief center—that is, before beginning an even more unlikely media career assisting a consumer reporter at a local TV station. "Rose, too, was a fairly easy character for us to create," Susan remembers, "because she sounded a lot like Katherine Helmond's character Jessica Tate from *Soap*."

Since Rose was to be of Scandinavian heritage, Susan borrowed the last name Nylund from a Swedish woman whom she and Paul had met while sailing the Yugoslav coast. "Rose was more Midwestern than prototypically Scandinavian," she says. "And there are a lot of names like that in the Midwest."

Blanche Devereaux

A GEORGIA PEACH who never fails to remind her roommates that she may still be a bit more ripe for the plucking, the hyper-sexual, uber-Southern widow Blanche is the owner of the house in which the Girls come to live—all the better to entertain a steady stream of gentleman callers. "Blanche was definitely the hardest character for us," Susan says. "We wanted very distinct characters, and that's why we placed their origins in different parts of the country." Problem was, Paul and Susan hailed from New York Yankee territory, and Tony Thomas grew up in Los Angeles, where his performer father Danny was based. So the trio turned to a reliable source: Southern literature.

"Blanche is almost a literary figure in representing that classic kind of Southern femininity," Paul explains. As Rue McClanahan remembers, Susan's pilot script describes the character as "more Southern than Blanche DuBois," her obvious namesake. "It's an homage," Paul says. "And certainly a way to remember which character was the Southern one," Susan adds. The trio decided to give Blanche the surname "Devereaux" to reflect the French influence in Louisiana and other parts of the Deep South.

Sophia Petrillo

AN ESCAPEE from the fire-ravaged Shady Pines nursing home, the eighty-something Sophia shows up at daughter Dorothy's door—and, in reality, because she immediately became so popular with viewing audiences, she never leaves. Sophia shows a tendency towards blunt honesty—caused, we're told, by a stroke that, sadly for her beleaguered daughter, destroyed the tactful part of her brain, yet left her with more than enough mobility to cause a great deal of trouble.

As former New Yorkers, Paul and Susan say they had grown up with Italian friends and neighbors, and liked the "New York sensibility," as Susan calls it, "either Italian or Jewish." "It's all very much the same," Paul adds, "except it's probably less clichéd to show an Italian-American mother/daughter duo than a Jewish one." Of course, their Brooklyn-bred Sicilian, Sophia, also knows her way around a knish, and her dialogue captures those cadences as well. Sophia exhibits the best of both backgrounds because, as the half-Sicilian and famously half-Lebanese Tony Thomas explains, "the funniest rhythms in the world are Semitic. Sophia was Italian, but she has a lot of the comedy rhythms I grew up with as well." In naming their pan-Mediterranean creation, Susan turned to her own childhood in Mount Vernon, New York, where a real family named Petrillo "is a large part of Mount Vernon history."

Age Before Beauty, Brains, and Naïveté

WHEN IT came time to find actresses to embody the four ladies they had created, the Witt-Thomas-Harris team, working with casting director Judith Weiner, knew they had plenty of talented, and unfortunately underemployed, sixty-something actresses to choose from. And so they focused their attention first on the character they felt would be hardest to find: feisty octogenarian Sophia Petrillo.

Estelle Getty had been primarily a stage actress in local productions in her home borough of Queens, New York, a late bloomer who had only recently scored her most noteworthy role playing the mother of Harvey Fierstein's Arnold Beckoff character in the playwright's initially off-off-Broadway production of *Torch Song Trilogy*. As she made a name for herself in Los Angeles during the show's subsequent West Coast run, Estelle landed some small Hollywood roles, including a blink-and-you'll-miss-it appearance in the film *Tootsie* (costarring Doris Belack, who played her future TV daughter Gloria Petrillo) and a larger role in the made-for-TV Western movie (Picture it: Estelle Getty?! In a *Western*?!), *No Man's Land*, with Stella Stevens. After the end of *Torch Song*'s 1984 run, Estelle returned to New York. Never believing that true Hollywood stardom could ever come to a self-described "little girl from the Lower East Side," she made a deal with her new manager Juliet Green to come back to Los Angeles for only two months during the following spring of 1985. And by the end of that time, Estelle had nailed the role of a lifetime.

Allison Jones, who was at the time a casting associate working with casting director Judith Weiner, remembers that Estelle had auditioned for Judith on February 8, 1985, for the guest starring role of Michael Gross's character's visiting mother on NBC's *Family Ties*. Judith had seen Estelle in *Torch Song*, but "It was the first time I'd ever heard of her," Allison remembers. "I even misspelled her name *Geddys* on the call sheet, and I never do that if I know someone." Estelle never got to join TV's Keaton family—she didn't get the part—but Judith remembered admiring her talent when it came time, a few weeks later, to cast her next project.

Although Susan Harris says that she created the character of Sophia Petrillo with no physical type in mind, Juliet and Estelle remember hearing that the *Golden Girls* producers were looking for a stereotypical "big, fat Italian mama with a bun." As Estelle writes in her 1988 memoir *If I Knew Then What I Know Now… So What?* she thought at first she would be reading for the role of Dorothy, and was surprised to hear she was to be considered for 80-year-old Sophia. Still, age and ethnic she could do—she had played those things before. Even "fat I knew I could handle." When she confessed to her TV writer friend Joel Kimmel that she doubted she was right for the part, he encouraged her to " 'do what you do best—make 'em laugh,'" Estelle writes. "I would play Sophia my way. I would play her New York Brooklyn."

I'm Older Than Dirt

ALLISON JONES remembers that Estelle had an amazing first "Sophia" audition for Judith Weiner in late February 1985. "She came in, so tiny, and she just was this character she was starting to create. I remember the way she said, 'I'm older than dirt!' with her New York accent. She made it her own, and nailed it to the extent that it was a no-brainer that we were going to take her to the producers, and hopefully in to read for the network."

Tony Thomas recalls that on the day the producers, who had "read a lot of people for Sophia but hadn't come close yet," were seeing another group of candidates, Paul and Susan were off working on one of the company's other shows. "Estelle came in to see me, and it was actually frightening—you don't expect to hear the words jump off the page that way," Tony says. "It was like, 'Oh my God, this is everything we wanted!'" He set up a callback for Estelle to come in to see his fellow producers as well as the pilot's director, Jay Sandrich. "I told them if you don't like her, have her do it again. Don't let her out of the room until you're satisfied, because she's the one."

In her book, Estelle remembers that the audition process ended up taking over a month. "The producers seemed pleased, but there was also a reservation: they thought I might be too young." Estelle got callback after callback—"I had never auditioned that many times for one role." And each time, as she met with more and different people, she was advised—don't change a thing. "I kept wondering, *if they don't want me to change anything, then why do they keep asking me back*?" Estelle remembers. Finally, Juliet got word that Estelle had made it to the final level: reading for the network. What neither woman knew, though, was that by now, Estelle was the only candidate being considered.

It's All About the Right Purse

AS SHE CONTINUED building the character of Sophia Petrillo for her big audition, Estelle decided she needed some props. "The quintessential bargain shopper," as

Juliet admiringly calls her, Estelle scoured the thrift stores of L.A.'s Fairfax district, searching for Sophia-like items: a size 12 polyester dress, lace-up orthopedic shoes, a straw hat with veil, gloves, and above all, a purse. "She was very insistent about finding the right purse," Juliet remembers. And indeed, the one Estelle ended up picking out is the famous straw, top-clasping bag which her character toted around for all of the show's seven seasons—the wardrobe department even ended up having a double made, in case of emergency. "She knew that a woman that age would have her medicines, her money, her whole life in her purse. So the purse was the key element that helped her get into character."

Juliet hired a makeup man to age Estelle's face and spray gray onto her hair. "From the time she walked through the doors at NBC and entered the waiting room, she was in character," Juliet remembers. "She walked in and said, 'Hello,' and they just fell apart." Warren Littlefield agrees. "When that little woman had those barbs hurling out of her mouth, it was like, excuse me, but I have to run down to the bathroom—I have no bodily control whatsoever," he enthuses. "When we saw that, we didn't care what the original inspiration was as far as physical type. Estelle was sensational and hilarious."

That very night, Estelle writes, she was at work on a television movie, *Copacabana* with Barry Manilow, being consoled by the *mensch*-y singer because she was convinced that the network would never choose her. And then Juliet got the call: Estelle was to be Sophia, the mothering influence to three somewhat younger women, yet to be chosen.

BEING A FRIEND: A CONVERSATION WITH JO DEWINTER

PAUL WITT and Susan Harris had originally read me for both Blanche and Rose, but by the time I was called to the network, it was only for Blanche. As I recall, I saw Blanche as slightly less flirtatious Southern belle, less "men are so cute," and more pragmatically aggressive. But that's probably because I'm physically very different from Rue—at five feet eight, I'm not small and darling in any way.

Still, over the years, Rue and I have often read for the same roles—I've gotten some of them and she's gotten some. That day, after the network reading, I walked out to the parking lot with Betty and Rue, and I said to Rue, who was my competition, "My heart sank when I saw you there," because I think she's such a terrific actress. "Why couldn't it have been someone I know I'm a great deal better than?!" We giggled a great deal about that.

As you know, I didn't get the part—much to my sorrow, I might add. I will admit that at first I was cranky and thought, "Well, if I didn't get it, then I don't want to watch it." That lasted for about two episodes, because I adore how they presented the idea that seemed so new then, that "women of a certain age" could be so vital. Plus, I knew it was incredibly funny. Susan Harris has the rare gift of being able to write some very sarcastic material without being mean.

Now, as I've watched the millions in residuals fade away, I've consoled myself that I didn't get the part because of my height and deep voice—I may have been too much like Bea. At least I like to think those were the deciding factors, because those are things I can't do a great deal about, whereas I would regret it if I hadn't given a great reading. But that day I feel I brought to it everything that I wanted to. After that, it's in the lap of the gods.

A Rose Is a Rose Is a... Blanche?

WITH THEIR Sophia in place, the production team concentrated on finding ladies to play her three younger roommates. They ran casting sessions in New York and Los Angeles, and as Paul Witt remembers, "saw a lot of talented actresses. Anyone of a certain age who saw the script wanted to do it."

Actress Jo DeWinter, who had auditioned for Witt-Thomas-Harris for the role of Mary Campbell on *Soap* and eventually appeared as a gynecologist in several episodes of that series, was among those who made it through several rounds of tryouts. Instructed to prepare to read for both Rose and Blanche, Jo says she had a unique perspective on just how good the pilot's writing was. "I thought, 'This is heaven,'" she remembers. "For the first time in a long time, this was witty material—not just setup-punch line. These were real people."

Eventually, as the producers and network executives narrowed their list from so many available choices, they decided to cast along traditional lines, picking actresses already known for particular qualities. At the time, Betty White was most famous for her recurring 1973–77 appearances on *The Mary Tyler Moore Show* as Minneapolis's happy homemaker-slash-neighborhood nymphomaniac Sue Ann Nivens. "She had played that part brilliantly on *Mary*," Paul explains, "and so we knew she could play Blanche. We didn't know if she could do the Southern thing, but we had to assume she could do anything, she's so good."

Rue McClanahan, on the other hand, was best known to TV audiences for a string of meeker roles: as put-upon second-banana neighbor Vivian Harmon on CBS's *Maude* and at the time as mousy Aunt Fran on NBC's less-than-stellar sitcom *Mama's Family*. (Having originally been promised a feistier character, Rue was miserable playing a woman so dull, and wanted out; Aunt Fran finally choked to death on a chicken bone in an early 1985 episode, leaving the actress just enough time to pursue a *Golden Girls* role.) The casting team zeroed in on Rue for Rose, realizing, as Paul notes, that even if the role was at the time not as deeply written, "Rue was someone who had always worked well in great ensembles, and had always carved out a really unique territory for herself."

Both Betty and Rue had crossed paths with the Witt-Thomas-Harris key players before. Betty knew Jay Sandrich from their time working together on *The Mary Tyler Moore Show*. Rue had also auditioned for, then won and turned down *Soap*'s Mary Campbell role, which eventually went to Cathryn Damon; she had her heart set on playing Mary's sister Jessica Tate, but that part already belonged to Katherine Helmond. Similarly, when Rue excitedly told her agent that she loved the *Golden Girls* pilot script and was thrilled to audition for the part of Blanche, she was devastated to hear she would be considered only for Rose. "My agent told me that they had Betty White in mind for the Blanche part already, and my heart sank," Rue remembers. "I said, 'How could I go to work every day playing Rose?' because I knew instinctively that I was just too right for Blanche. And she said, 'Well, it's either that, or you don't do the series at all.'"

The Golden Switch

NOT WILLING to give up being part of a show she knew could make TV history—"I knew from the moment I opened the envelope and saw *The Golden Girls* written on the cover in cursive typeface that it would be a hit," she claims—Rue acquiesced: she would play Rose. But then, on her first meeting with the pilot's director, *Mary Tyler Moore Show* and *Soap* veteran Jay Sandrich, something historic happened. After her reading of Rose, "Jay said, 'I'm going to do something unorthodox—would you mind reading Blanche for me?'" Rue remembers. "And I said, 'If you insist.' I knew that he must have seen what I saw and known what I knew, and he needed to see if it worked."

"I had never met Rue," Jay explains. "And I didn't really watch *Maude*, so I didn't know how good she was. After she read Rose, I said to her, 'You're really wonderful—but I don't for one second believe you're innocent.'"

A few days later, when Rue and Betty came in to read for the director together, Jay had the same surprise for Betty—knowing from their years together on *The Mary Tyler Moore Show* that "she can get a laugh doing anything," he asked her to read for Rose. "Betty had had no inkling," Rue says. "And then her eyes widened and she said, 'Rose?!'"

Betty remembers how Jay broke the news to her: he felt that if she were to play another nymphomaniac, no matter what small changes she made, the audience was going to think it was Sue Ann all over again. "But at that point I knew who Blanche was, but I didn't know who Rose was at all," Betty remembers. Susan Harris told Betty that Rose was actually her favorite character—which Betty suspected just might be a ploy to bring her around to agreeing to the switch. "But then the more I looked at Rose, the more I was okay with it," she explains. "And I give Jay Sandrich full credit for helping me make it work. He said Rose doesn't have a sarcastic bone in her body, that she isn't witty, or hip at all. She takes every single word literally and puts them all together and it makes perfect sense for her. And when he said that, it made sense for me."

And so, the qualities that had originally gotten each actress in the door were now thrown out the window. Rue was to be mousy no more, and Betty was to take a break from the man-baiting business. "Betty was hysterical as Rose," Rue says. "Her eyes went wide and stayed that way for seven years. I used to call them her Little Orphan Annie eyes—white ovals with nothing in them. The irony is that she's such an incredibly brilliant woman. But she did that so well and was so funny at it."

"And Rue took Blanche and went with her where I never would have had the guts to go," Betty adds. "So it just worked out beautifully."

A Bea Arthur Type

NOW, THE last of the women left to cast was Dorothy, ostensibly the lead role within the ensemble. Susan had created the character with only one person in mind—she had even described the character in her stage directions as "a Bea Arthur type." The problem was, Bea wasn't interested.

Susan, who had worked with Bea on *Maude*—in fact, she wrote that series' most famous episode, "Maude's Abortion"—and on *Soap*, where Bea played God in a fourth season episode, had her heart set. But with the actress refusing the role, the team was forced to move on. And so, like any good gay boy would do, NBC's Senior Vice President of Talent and Casting Joel Thurm suggested a Broadway favorite. As Joel recalls, "I said to Brandon Tartikoff, there's one other woman who I think would be very good for this. And she has a lot of the same rough edges, and she's new—no one has seen her on television, other than a British series she did for a while. Her name is Elaine Stritch."

Brandon Tartikoff and Judith Weiner both agreed that auditioning Elaine Stritch would be a good idea. But it took not only until after striking a "test deal" with Stritch's agent and arranging her plane ticket and hotel room, but until the moment when Elaine entered Joel's executive-filled office at NBC for her audition, that he learned just how much Susan was stuck on casting Bea. And only Bea.

And Then There's... Elaine Stritch?

JOEL'S LARGE NBC office, where Elaine's audition took place, sat sixteen people around an L-shaped couch, and "On a good day, the vibes for an actor, looking at all those faces, could be horrendous," he explains. "But that day, because Susan and Paul and Tony and some other people had the agenda in mind of accepting only Bea, the room was ice cold. Add to that, of the NBC people, not everybody knew who Elaine Stritch was. Then when she started to read, she was really nervous and she had a couple of misstarts. Then her reading started out okay, but it got zero reaction. So what happens to a performer when there's no reaction in the room? They start getting bigger and bigger. It ended up being a disaster."

It was then, in that room, that Susan Harris revealed to NBC that she had written the part expressly for Bea. The problem was, never mind Bea's feelings about the role—NBC didn't want her anyway. Brandon Tartikoff worried that Bea's "Q" scores, which track a performer's standing amongst audience members, were exceedingly low. "She had a very high familiarity, like 80 or 90 percent," Joel explains. But undoubtedly because of *Maude*'s unabashed liberalism and TV abortion, "of those who knew her, only 20 percent liked her." For weeks, all through the early development phases of *The Golden Girls*, Tartikoff had been adamant: no Bea

Arthur. But now that the Elaine Stritch plan had fizzled, there was no Plan B (or would that be, Plan Bea?)

Finally, as the discussion in the room became heated, Susan and Paul began to make some headway with the network president. They argued that unlike *Maude*, *The Golden Girls* would be an ensemble piece. The show would not rest solely on Bea's shoulders, and there would be three other women who could win over anyone Maude Findlay had possibly alienated. Finally, the network chief gave in.

Maude and Vivian, Meet Sue Ann Nivens

EVEN WITH NBC on board with Bea, Susan Harris still had to convince the actress to accept the part of Dorothy Zbornak. So she prevailed upon Bea's former *Maude* castmate Rue McClanahan to put the pressure on. And so Rue called Bea, and "I said, 'Why on earth are you turning down the best script that's ever going to come across your desk as long as you live?'" Rue says. "And she said, 'Rue, I have no interest in playing Maude and Vivian meet Sue Ann Nivens.' I said, 'That's not the way we're going to play it, Bea. I'm going to play the Sue Ann Nivens vamp, and Betty's going to play the Vivian role.' And Bea took a beat and said, 'Now THAT is very interesting.'" With that, the team was set. "And next thing you know, the four of us, including Estelle, came in to read for the suits at NBC. And we laid them low. And THAT's the way they cast it."

BEING A FRIEND: A CONVERSATION WITH ELAINE STRITCH

I'M NEVER impressed with sitcoms. They're not my kind of thing. I don't think my humor fits sitcoms, either. But I went out to L.A. and auditioned for *The Golden Girls*, and I tell the story in my one-woman show *Elaine Stritch at Liberty* what the meeting was like.

I met a room full of people who were just stonewalled against me, and it was terrifying and not pleasant. Before I started to read, I tried to explain that there was some of the dialogue that didn't sit comfortably with me. And I said, "If you don't mind, I'd like to change a few things." And Susan Harris said, "Hopefully just the punctuation." And I thought, "I'm up against something here." Well, her answer didn't sit well with me, and I guess the devil came up in me. So I said, "For example, on page seven where Dorothy says, 'Don't forget the hors d'oeuvres,' do you mind if I say 'the *fucking* hors d'oeuvres?' Well, that made her mad.

The whole thing didn't go down very well, and I was very nervous. Cut to the chase, it was so the right thing to happen. *The Golden Girls* and I did not fit. First of all, the idea really didn't appeal to me at all—three broads living together in Florida? What could be less exciting? But in retrospect, I do think the show turned out excellent—and it's amazing the life it's had. And I'm so glad it happened to Bea, making her life certainly a lot more luxurious. But I think if I'd have gotten the part and been stuck out there in LA, doing a sitcom for seven years, I might never have sobered up.

I think we can all look back in retrospect and realize that most things that happen to us happen because they're meant to. So we have to accept them one day at a time. And I get a lot of mileage from this story in my show because *The Golden Girls* is such a popular thing, and I treat my own hurt feelings about it with humor. I get laughs in the theater, and so the whole experience has served its purpose and given me what I needed—a good piece of writing in my show coming out of a very bad experience.

Just remember when you relay this story in your book, make me sound classy. I try always to be classy, and it's fucking hard.

And Then There's Bea

FOR HER part, Bea doesn't remember having hesitated based on Betty and Rue's roles; she says she simply must have been the last person in town to get her hands on the *Golden Girls* pilot script. "I got a phone call from my agent who said, 'What's this I hear about you doing a new show?' I told him I had no idea what he was talking about, and he said there was a new show I was cast in," Bea remembers. "I told him, I know nothing about it, and nobody is calling me. A few days after, I did get a script, and found out that everybody in the country had auditioned for a part described as 'a Bea Arthur type.'" Luckily for TV history, Bea sat down with the script and read it. "I have gotten very lazy," she admits, "and I don't want to work if I don't think a script is fabulous. And this was a fabulous script."

Bea's contract paperwork was rushed to her house just in time on that Good Friday, April 5. The cast began rehearsals the following Monday, April 8. There was now no time to lose in fleshing out Susan Harris's leading ladies. Because just nine days later on Wednesday, April 17, 1985, *The Golden Girls*'s pilot was scheduled to be videotaped at Los Angeles's Sunset Gower Studios in front of a live studio audience.

Casting Coco

BUT WAIT—there was still one more character yet to be cast—remember that gay houseboy? He was now named Coco—after Susan Harris's dog. And he was playing it quite hard to get.

Golden Girls casting associate Allison Jones notes that the many candidates for Coco ranged all over the Kinsey Scale, including her friend Dom Irrera and another Italian-American comic actor, Paul Provenza— both of whom in real life certainly display far more hetero swagger than swish.

Early on, the producers began eyeing Jeffrey Jones— no relation to Allison—who had recently played a young, gay Brit in a New York run of Caryl Churchill's play

Cloud Nine, an effete emperor in the 1984 film *Amadeus*, and was generating buzz for his upcoming, soon-to-be-infamous role as Matthew Broderick's nemesis Principal Rooney in 1986's *Ferris Bueller's Day Off*. But as he remembers, Jeffrey spoiled his chances himself.

"I wasn't concerned about playing another gay character," Jeffrey explains, "but I didn't think this character was very realistic, but more cheap; obvious and jokey. When I went in to read, they asked what I thought, and I naively told them: I thought that Coco brought the show in the wrong direction, away from the women. He didn't fit with the interplay of the characters and so he just seemed unnecessary. I guess I talked myself out of a job."

Although both Susan Harris and Allison Jones say that there had never been an age or particular "type" at all in mind for Coco, both Paul Provenza and Jeffrey Jones recall having been told that the show's casting team was at one point thinking of Coco as a drag queen. "But they wanted an actor doing drag, not a drag queen trying to act," Paul recalls. "Still, they weren't sure an actor could really commit to being a drag queen. I said, 'Let me think about it and let you know.'" With a plan in mind, Paul was referred through a mutual friend to actress/writer Hillary Carlip, who was at the time the lead singer of the band she had formed, Angel and the Reruns. "Her entire garage was filled with all kinds of costumes," Paul remembers. "So I went to her house and picked out something I thought would work. Hillary decked me out, and a friend of ours did makeup. Rather than coming off like a big, flamboyant drag queen, I chose to look like a guy who's trying to pass for a nice, average, Beverly Hills–esque woman."

Never having done drag before, Paul showed up on the studio lot for his audition "and was having the damnedest time in those fucking heels." But his look was convincing—maybe too convincing. "As I was leaving, I was talking to the casting people, whom I knew quite well. All the while, I was thinking they knew exactly who I was and were just playing along. Finally, I revealed it was me, and they couldn't believe it. Plus, on the way back to my car, I got hit on by the lot's security guard, who said, 'I've never seen you around here before. You must be new in town,' which I thought was really funny. So I didn't get the part, but I did have a fun time doing the audition."

Paul Witt remembers that the search for just the right actor to play Coco became harder than the producers had originally envisioned. "We wanted an actor who could play gay life with dignity," he explains. "That's very tricky." And, again at odds with Jones's and Provenza's memories of the producers casting for drag queens, Paul explains, "We didn't want to get laughs out of outrageous, campy stuff." When it came to finding the actor who could deliver all that, he says, demographics didn't matter. "It never occurred to us to cast a straight guy versus a gay guy. We just knew that we wanted the character to integrate in a way that he would be part of this family."

Enter Charles Levin

IT WAS NBC president Brandon Tartikoff who suggested Charles Levin, who three years earlier had begun a groundbreaking recurring gay role on the network's Emmy-winning drama *Hill Street Blues*. Charles's character Eddie Gregg was a flamboyant men's room hustler who forms an unlikely, soul-matching friendship with Bruce Weitz's otherwise solitary detective Belker. Eddie first appeared in the show's third season opener "Trial By Fury," which won the 1982 Emmy for Outstanding Writing in a Drama Series and a Humanitas award for the show's creator David Milch. The network took notice. And when they needed another gay character, they went back to Charles Levin.

Charles remembers that when he first met with the *Golden Girls* pilot's Jay Sandrich, he was surprised at the director's resistance to the same gay affectations that had worked so well in the Eddie role. "Jay told me, 'I don't want you coming in here, doing a lisp or mincing around,'" Charles remembers. "He did not want the character to be flamboyant at all—just a regular guy who was gay. The trouble was, that wasn't what was written on the page. Susan Harris had written that he was a 'fancy man,' as Sophia still calls him in the pilot to this day. And his lines were outrageous, hilarious and way over the top."

Charles was unnerved, but tried to follow Jay's direction. "But it really threw a wrench into my plans," he says. "I didn't feel comfortable just coming in and 'playing it straight'—I needed that mask of whatever I chose to do to portray a gay person." When he had his big reading for the network in Brandon's office, Charles read the lines as Jay had specified. "And there wasn't a peep in the house. They looked at me like, 'What the

Sharing Cheesecake with Betty White

Q QUOTE: *Speaking of sharing cheesecake: I love cheesecake, but I never eat on camera—I just toy with it. But ask Rue about what she does. Because I'm telling you, if it's on camera, it's a license to steal, as far as Rue is concerned. It has no calories. So she'd not only eat the cheesecake, but when Sophia would make spaghetti, she'd eat that, too.*

AS AN ACTOR, you get so many bad scripts, but when I read the pilot script for *The Golden Girls*, I sat up and took notice. It was different from anything I'd gotten. And it was all because of the wonderful writing. The four of us get a lot of credit, but we couldn't do it if it weren't for the amazing scripts. I promise you, as an actor you can screw up a good show, but you can't save a bad one if it's not on the page.

From the first table read of the script, we knew we were onto something. Everyone was so perfectly cast that the minute you heard the lines coming out of our mouths, it was exciting—I've never had a read-through like that. All of a sudden, I'd start throwing them over the net, and I'd get them right back. We all had the same reaction. We could feel the chemistry. We could taste it.

The magic of the show was the way the writers drew our characters so distinctly— all these years I've used the analogy of four points on a compass. We balanced each other out beautifully. And not only were the lines wonderful, but they would shoot the reactions of the other characters. So pretty soon, since the audience got to know these women so well, they'd start to anticipate, 'Oh, how is Bea going to react to that?' Or Rue, or Estelle. It made for a very exciting seven years.

I always believed that Rose was truly naïve more than dumb. I'd hear people calling her ditzy or a dumbbell, and I would defend her. Of course, she did think her second grade teacher was Adolf Hitler, so it was a very fine line. In playing Rose, I found that the most interesting challenge was that, even though as an actor I had to kind of think funny and play on things in my head, I had to be careful to keep the awareness not only out of my mouth but also out of my eyes. Rose couldn't ever look like she got it. She had to be innocence personified. That was the saving grace that would allow her to get away with saying something like "Can you believe that backstabbing slut?" about Blanche. Those were the lines where the producers would warn me, "You never get it. You're never too smart for the room." They knew that coming from Rose the line would work, but coming from Betty it wouldn't.

Rose is like Betty in some ways, in her optimism and her wanting to think that life always has a happy ending. That was in the script, so I don't think I brought that to the role, but it was just something that was terribly comfortable for me. She also has a Viking temper—like me, I'm afraid—and wasn't always sweetness and light. When she got mad, she got really mad. But Betty isn't as prone to telling someone off. No point in getting into a confrontation—I'll just wait until they go home and then I'll bitch like mad.

From the start, 75 percent of our mail has always come from young people, especially in their teens and early twenties. Fans will often come up to me and quote every line of a St. Olaf story, and I don't blame them—they were brilliant. When I'd read a script and see one, I'd be thrilled. I don't do accents, but there was just an undulating rhythm to those words that I was able to pick up on. Still, sometimes before work if I'd see a newspaper story with some very difficult-to-pronounce Scandinavian name, I'd think uh-oh—I'm going to get it. And sure enough, it would show up in the script. I swear the other girls would make bets that I'd never make it through some of these difficult words. So when I told a St. Olaf story, I always had to look over their shoulders instead of locking eyes with any of them. Because I knew they were just sitting there, thinking, "You're going to screw up—you know you are!"

When the show premiered we were at number one, over Bill Cosby, who at that time owned the world. We felt, well, that's just curiosity, that first show—four old broads are not going to continue to get that kind of ratings. Well, we stayed, and I don't think we were ever out of the top ten, which is such a privilege. It was just one of those things that comes along—I would say once in a lifetime, but my "once in a lifetime" had already been used up with *Mary Tyler Moore*. So to get it again—and even now, on *Boston Legal*, with David E. Kelley's writing, I mean, how lucky can one old broad get?

hell are you doing? This isn't funny.' And they said, dismissively, 'Thank you very much.'"

Charles left the audition convinced that he had blown it, and angry with Jay Sandrich for what had turned out to be bad advice. "They had chosen me based on a prior character, and Jay wouldn't let me play anything like that character," he remembers. Later that night, Charles got a call at home from NBC's VP of Casting Joel Thurm. "He said, 'We don't know what you were doing, but would you please come back tomorrow and just play Eddie Gregg?' So the next day I went back and did Eddie Gregg. And with the first word out of my mouth, these people were in stitches. I had put the mask back in place, and was playing the character I enjoyed playing. And given the lines, which were so brilliant, it just worked. And I got hired right then and there."

CHAPTER THREE

Curtain Up

QUOTE

Normally with new shows, they take only a few minutes' worth of clips to New York to show the advertisers each May. But with *The Golden Girls*, they decided to show the whole pilot. And from what I've been told, the audience in the grand ballroom at the Waldorf-Astoria hotel laughed so loud that they ended up missing some of the lines. Five minutes after it finished, my phone rang, and it was my friend Grant Tinker, who was then at NBC. He said, 'Betty, don't make any plans for the next couple of years. I think you're going to be very busy.'"

–Betty White

ON THE NIGHT of April 17, 1985, as *The Golden Girls* was taping its pilot episode, it was immediately evident to all involved that a potential classic—and certainly a show with the potential to run for years—was being born.

In fact, the producers had known even earlier that they were onto something special. Something that would normally be considered once-in-a-lifetime, except in Susan Harris's case, after *Soap*, it was now happening twice. From the first time the pilot script was read aloud around a rehearsal table, Paul Witt says, "Everyone there, from the performers to the craft service guy to the network to us, knew it was a home run." It was evident that all of the elements needed for a great TV show—great script, great cast—had fallen precisely into place.

The Witt-Thomas-Harris sitcom methodology, developed over the decade-long span of shows like *Fay*, *Soap*, and *Benson*, called for two tapings of any given episode, in front of two separate live audiences. The first show, referred to as the "dress show," was used to work out any remaining kinks; if something fell flat, it could be rewritten during dinner, where the cast could be given new lines to perform at the "air show" later that evening. *The Golden Girls* pilot worked this same way—the episode was actually taped twice, in front of two different audience groups. And both audiences went wild for it.

Jay Sandrich remembers the audience's huge laughter that night when, as the actresses had cooked up on stage that week, Dorothy put Rose in a chokehold, to keep her from blabbing to Blanche her suspicions about the true nature of her intended husband. And there was an even bigger explosion when Sophia shockingly summed up the situation with a simple, "The man is a douchebag!" (an epithet that ultimately had to be re-shot as "scuzzbag" before NBC's censors would allow it to air).

The show's producers were not surprised to hear the reaction to unfiltered and outrageous persona. According to Jay, Estelle had been getting such big laughs from the start that she had inspired a change to the structure of the show: now, instead of Sophia living at Shady Pines, and making only recurring appearances on the show, she would be a regular character, living with the three other girls after Shady Pines burns down. Sophia was now a full member of the family.

… and It's Curtains for Coco

AS FORTUITOUS as Sophia's promotion was for Estelle, and for the eventual formula of the show, it ultimately spelled curtains for Coco. As Charles Levin remembers of the pilot taping night, "old pros" Rue, Betty, and Bea brought down the house as expected. But when Estelle, the one unknown among the ladies, came in, "They didn't know what to make of her, and they fell in love with her." That night, not only did Estelle Getty hold her own playing against three television heavyweights, but "she sandbagged everybody. During the rehearsal, she was insecure. But like the true stage pro she is, when the lights went up and the audience was there, Estelle was on fire. The woman couldn't miss, and everybody saw it. It wasn't, 'Did you see what Estelle did?' It was, 'Oh my God, Estelle is stealing the show out from under three real comic pros.'"

Meanwhile, the pilot's audience had gone cuckoo for Coco, too. As Charles explains, "They'd never seen a character like him. They'd seen characters flirt with being gay or hint at it. But this guy, as soon as he opened his mouth, was way out there. So far out there, they found it hilarious and endearing." But with four other characters also getting big laughs, the house at 5161 Richmond Street was getting a little too crowded.

All week, as the actors prepared for the pilot taping, Charles remembers Estelle's lack of confidence. "She and I gravitated toward one another because we were the lesser-knowns," he recalls. "She was certain she was going to be fired. She said, 'If it's between you and me, Chuck, you're obviously staying. I'm gone.' I didn't see it that way, and rehearsals were going so well, I didn't have those worries."

But after the taping, when the supposedly twenty-three-ish minute pilot clocked in at over twenty-eight minutes, some painful cuts had to be made. "Everybody lost stuff," Paul Witt explains. And although it might be tempting to wonder whether, in the height of the AIDS panic in 1985, Coco might have been cut to appease an already *Love, Sidney*-scarred NBC, everyone involved with *The Golden Girls* insists that the character was eliminated purely for artistic and practical reasons.

"It really came down to that there wasn't enough room in a half hour," Paul explains. "Charles Levin was a terrific actor, and was terrific in the part, but we had too much." As Susan Harris adds, "We couldn't possibly service all five regular characters adequately. It would have been unfair." Perhaps finally seeing Jeffrey Jones's earlier point about Coco's storylines being somewhat off-topic, the producers decided to whittle the show's focus down to its very core—the relationships among just the four women.

Paul explains that in justifying the painful decision to themselves, the team admitted that maybe it wasn't a good idea anyway to have someone working for the Girls; without some housework to busy themselves with during scenes, all the actresses would be doing was sitting. And for a show supposedly about the struggles of older women living together partly out of economic need, a live-in houseboy might suggest that they were too comfortably well off. "We wanted people to identify with them," Susan says. "We needed the element of struggle so that the audience would worry about them."

Warren Littlefield says that, far from being worried about any backlash due to airing a show with a gay character, he was actually a little reluctant to let Coco

CELEBRITY SURVEY #2:

WHEN AND WITH WHOM DID YOU FIRST WATCH THE *GIRLS*?

FROM THE START, thank you. And I'm offended that you would even ask. I even remember the gay houseboy/cook. But I could never make it through an episode of *Empty Nest*, which *The Golden Girls* was paired with, because I have standards.

-Tony Tripoli, actor,
My Network TV's *Fashion House*

IN RERUNS. I had a boyfriend who loved the show back in the 1990s but I didn't get into it then.
–Keith Boykin, BET TV show host

IN RERUNS, when various boyfriends who were huge fans made me watch it.
-Ben Patrick Johnson,
author of *One Size Fits All*

IN RERUNS on KTLA in Los Angeles in the mid-nineties. At the time, I lived with four other guys and we would eat breakfast and watch the Girls.

-Bruce Daniels, comic

1985. I had just moved to New York to become an actor, and I remember seeing them on the cover of *TV Guide* in an A&P in Brooklyn. It described these old ladies as "middle aged." Middle aged? Who lives to be 120? I also remember thinking, "It will never be as big as *Night Court*."

-Craig Chester,
actor/writer/director of *Adam & Steve*

1991, after I moved to LA, and I kept getting tickets to go see tapings of the show. Then I'd watch in re-runs, mostly with my boyfriend Don. We LOVED the show.

-Dan Bucatinsky, actor/writer/producer

1991, when I moved to LA from Boston and my friends here would not leave the house on Saturday night until after *The Golden Girls* were off. I thought they were insane to be so hooked on a show about over-the-hill white women. Then I sat down and watched it and said, "Ohhh."

-Doug Spearman, actor

IN RERUNS. During the original run I was in my twenties living in New York. I was more interested in blond muscle boys than Golden Girls.

-Bob Smith, writer/stand-up comedian

DURING ITS ORIGINAL RUN. I did not have a car for the first half of it, so it was by default that I watched the show. But it wasn't until its reincarnation on Lifetime that I became a real fan. I heard so many references from my friends and had to see what the fuss was all about.

-Jermaine Taylor, panelist, GSN's *I've Got a Secret*

DURING ITS ORIGINAL RUN, and I rediscovered it during reruns on Lifetime. It was a very important activity that I did with my boyfriend at the time. It was the only half hour that we could agree on anything. And when they aired two back to back...well, we were almost perfect for a whole hour!

-Ari Gold, musician and DJ

DURING ITS ORIGINAL RUN. In fact, I was dating someone who was in LA and happened to have been at the taping of the PILOT! He came back to Boston screaming about what an amazing show it was going to be—and he was right. (Whatever happened to him?)

-Billy Masters, syndicated columnist and performer

FROM THE BEGINNING, because they were on Saturday night and it was what you did when you didn't have a date—which most often I didn't. I remember when I was doing a show in Cincinnati, I was making some new friends in a gay bar and one of them referred to another guy as a real "friend of Dorothy." I told him I thought it was amazing that after all these years we were still talking about Judy Garland. He quickly corrected me and told me he was talking about Bea Arthur.

–Jaffe Cohen, stand-up comedian
and author of the novel *Tush*

FROM THE BEGINNING. I was in my twenties and it was the hottest show then. We would be at a huge New York party and it would shut down for the half hour. And then afterward, everyone would go back to what they were doing. Lesbos and gay boys loved it and it became "our" show. We never missed it.

–Suzanne Westenhoefer, stand-up comedian
and panelist, GSN's *I've Got a Secret*

FROM THE BEGINNING, and I even taped them for posterity. Who knew they were going to invent the DVD?!

–Frank DeCaro, talk show host,
Sirius Satellite Radio and
panelist on GSN's *I've Got a Secret*

FROM THE PILOT, which I saw at a desert spa with my mother on a bonding weekend. We watched it through a veil of mud.

–Bruce Vilanch, writer/performer

FROM THE VERY FIRST EPISODE. My family would get together on Saturday nights and we'd watch. There is nothing funnier than raunchy old broads trashing each other.

—Derek Hartley, talk-show host, Sirius Satellite Radio

FROM THE VERY BEGINNING. My parents are from another country and don't watch a lot of English-language programming, so I would watch *The Golden Girls* all by myself and feel a little bit like I was doing something rather illicit.

—Rex Lee, actor, HBO's *Entourage*

FROM THE BEGINNING. I would watch with gays of course, like my friends Steve and Blain, and sometimes my grandmother, who spoke only Greek. I remember thinking if my Greek grandmother could get such a kick out of this show, it's really something special.

—ANT, stand-up comedian and host of VH1's *Celebrity Fit Club*

DURING ITS ORIGINAL RUN. I watched it mostly alone, but sometimes with my mother. I didn't like to miss an episode.

—Tammy Etheridge, actress/writer

FROM THE BEGINNING, when I used to watch with my mother. My mother stopped watching after a few years because she felt the Girls were becoming too catty to one another. I, on the other hand, lapped up every catty barb with sheer delight!

–Varla Jean Merman, cabaret performer and actress, *Girls Will Be Girls*

DURING THE ORIGINAL RUN, which I watched with my wonderful late grandmother Hazel, namesake of our fine home furnishings shop in my hometown of New Orleans. She was a vibrant steel magnolia who identified with the Girls and appreciated being represented on network TV.

–Bryan Batt, actor, *Jeffrey*

DURING THE ORIGINAL RUN, but I didn't really get hooked until it aired at seven every night. I would watch with my oldest gay friend, Jack, who died at 78. We would watch it together in his bed.

–John Bartlett, designer

DURING THE ORIGINAL RUN, with my best friend ever Jonathan Bixby, the Broadway costume designer who is now in heaven. Whenever someone would mention *The Golden Girls*, he would sing, to the tune of the theme song, "Thank you for oversized tops."

—Douglas Carter Beane, playwright

WHEN AND WITH WHOM DID YOU FIRST WATCH THE GIRLS?

go, but he eventually yielded to Paul Witt's logic about cutting the show for time. And so, through the use of some pickup shots filmed later and additional looped dialogue, *The Golden Girls*'s gay houseboy was carefully excised from as many scenes in the pilot as possible. And since this was the era before the advent of "TV on DVD" gift sets, with their lost scenes presented as "extras," most of Levin's work fell forever to the cutting room floor. Once on the verge of making TV history as a regular gay character, Coco had now instead gone the way of the dodo. When, a few months later, *The Golden Girls* resumed production for its first season, only the ladies were to return, and were destined quickly to gel into classic TV's First Foursome.

BEHIND THE SCENES: A CONVERSATION WITH COSTUME DESIGNER JUDY EVANS STEELE

IN DESIGNING clothes for *The Golden Girls*, I wanted to keep it overall feeling like Florida—bright, with lots of prints. But you do take some license. Even though it's hot in Florida, we didn't do sleeveless shirts because we wanted to be flattering to these older actresses. And I layered clothes to be flattering, even though you might not do that if it's a hundred degrees outside. I didn't worry about putting them in clothes it looked like they could afford, either. The main idea was to make the ladies look good. We didn't want this to be four dowdy ladies.

I wanted a sexy, soft, and flowing look for Rue, a tailored, pulled-together look for Bea, a sweet, down-home look for Betty, and comfort for Estelle. I custom-designed all of Blanche and Dorothy's clothes, but Rose and Sophia's were usually off-the-rack, with a lot of alterations to make them fit. It amounted to a lot of shopping and sewing, because often the ladies could have seven to ten costume changes per show.

The Golden Girls is definitely an '80s show. But looking back, I get the "What were we thinking?" feeling less than I would on other shows. A lot of those clothes you could probably get away with today. But yes, I definitely took chances, and remember—Bob Mackie could do the most stupendous design, and half the people will love it, half will hate it. You can't get everybody to agree. As a costume designer, you have a very short time to put these things together, and if you go out on a limb, you either make a wonderful statement or you end up doing something you wouldn't do again.

CHAPTER FOUR

What Made the Girls So Golden

QUOTE

"Back then, Saturday was a night where no one was dominating. So the way that Brandon looked at it was that we could dominate if we found the right shows. He thought that the reason the HUT [Households Using Television] level was down on Saturday was because nothing good was on."

—Garth Ancier, former head of current comedy at NBC

Saturday Night Dead

FROM THE NIGHT of its September 14, 1985, debut, *The Golden Girls* earned golden ratings—and did so on a night where successful comedies have been rarer than platinum. Although Saturday night had once been home to CBS's classic comedies of the 1970s—*The Mary Tyler Moore Show*, *The Bob Newhart Show*, *All in the Family*, and *The Carol Burnett Show*—that legendary lineup was broken up little by little as the powerhouse programs were shifted around to shore up the network's other flagging nights. By 1985, Saturday had been all but abandoned. So when they heard that their promising new show was to air Saturdays at 9:00 p.m., the producers of *The Golden Girls* initially feared the worst.

But NBC had research to justify the bold decision to begin building a comedy block on Saturday night, with the still-unproven *The Golden Girls* as its 9:00 p.m. tentpole. After all, the show's presumed target audience—the older set—is often the only group home during prime weekend partying hours. But through testing, the network had learned something else, too: beyond anyone's prediction, the pilot showed just as much appeal to just about all other age groups, too, including young adults, teens—even kids. *The Golden Girls*, test audiences predicted, would be an across-the-board hit. And with a hit early enough on Saturday night, NBC could draw people over 50 as they settled in for the night with the kids and grandkids, as well as those between 18 and 49 before they decided which movie to rent or which club to attend. And hopefully, the network could even keep them around all the way through the 1:00 a.m. end of *Saturday Night Live*.

Premiering just before cable, with its hundreds of channels and nothing on, proliferated in American households, *The Golden Girls* became one of the last of the old-school broadcast network hits. With little Saturday night competition, the *Girls* routinely drew a 30-plus "share," meaning that 30 percent or more of the television-viewing audience at the time was tuned into the show; producers of today's shows are ecstatic if they draw a share in the double digits. In all parts of the U.S.—red states and blue alike—*The Golden Girls* was a water-cooler hit. With Blanche's antics as likely to be discussed in New York as they were in New Mexico, the show was a force bringing America together, unifying people of varying demographics and geographics, if only for a half hour every Saturday night.

Golden Appeal:
Why People Love *The Golden Girls*

EVER SINCE *The Golden Girls* went off the air in 1992, Saturday night has been abandoned again. The broadcast networks have once again hung the "Gone Fishin'" sign on the night, airing no original scripted programming. But for so many of us who remember the show fondly today, *The Golden Girls* ushered in a Saturday night comedy tradition, a comfortable world of funny grandmas and cheesecake to snuggle into on a Saturday night. Harkening back to the wholesome early days of TV, here was a show about grandparents you could watch *with* your grandparents. It aired on a night when bedtimes were relaxed and extended families might be together. It was witty enough for adults, while kids, research showed, related to brash little Sophia.

For Generations X and Y, Blanche, Dorothy, Rose, and Sophia often became regular babysitters, seeing kids and young teens through Saturday nights at home while parents and older siblings might be out on dates; twenty years later for those grown-up kids, the show's six-times-daily repeats on the Lifetime cable network bring with them an air of nostalgia. For older viewers, *The Golden Girls* was the rare network show centered on relatable women "of a certain age," bringing dignity and visibility to an otherwise Madison Avenue– and thus network-ignored bracket.

But most importantly, the big draw for viewers of all ages was the show's impeccable writing. Working from a template designed by the revered Susan Harris, the show deftly managed the delicate balance of compelling, moving storytelling with razor-sharp jokes. As the only show on the air with such mature leads, *The Golden Girls* had the advantage of having certain subject areas all to itself—and it mined them brilliantly for every vein of their inherent humor. What other show could bring four old ladies to a nudist colony—and get away with wringing a laugh out of their every cringe? Or have them arrested as Miami's unlikeliest hookers? As it packed on the clever wordplay and double entendre, *The Golden Girls* far surpassed the IQ level of most of its 1980s peers—quick, try to think of your favorite smart joke from *Growing Pains*—and enticed veteran comedy writers and talented newcomers alike to join its writing staff. In fact, by the end of its run, the show had become a training ground for some of today's hottest writer/creators, including Mitchell Hurwitz of *Arrested Development* and Marc Cherry of *Desperate Housewives*.

The Power of Four

THE GOLDEN GIRLS defined a generation's view of older women, and single-handedly resurrected comedy during primetime on Saturday night. But perhaps the show's most lasting innovation is the comedy formula it pioneered. Call it the "Golden Rule of Four."

"Four points on a compass," as Betty White aptly describes them, the characters of Dorothy, Blanche, Rose, and Sophia match up to four classic comedic types: respectively, the Brain, the Slut, the Ditz, and the Big Mouth. Separately, none of them is anyone we haven't seen on a sitcom before; the power comes when you shack the four of them up together. For some indefinable reason, there's magic in the number four. Comedy duos are a classic tradition, but a completely different animal. And while it's certainly true that three women can work, especially in film—think *9 to 5*— having three lead characters in a sitcom might leave one of them having to carry the "B" plot on her own. Five can be too crowded—think the *Desperate Housewives* poker games when Edie joins in. Love her as we do, doesn't she sometimes seem like one self-involved slut too many? But four? Four leaves us with infinite possibilities. Rose takes Dorothy's night school class in

The Golden

The Golden Girls NBC 1985–92	Designing Women CBS 1986–93	Living Single FOX 1993–98
"Old"	"Southern"	"Black"
Dorothy (Bea Arthur)	Julia (Dixie Carter) & Mary Jo (Annie Potts)	Khadijah (Queen Latifah)
Sophia (Estelle Getty)	Anthony (Meshach Taylor)	Maxine (Erika Alexander)
Blanche (Rue McClanahan)	Suzanne (Delta Burke)	Regine (Kim Fields)
Rose (Betty White)	Charlene (Jean Smart)	Synclaire (Kim Coles)

Influence

Sex and the City HBO 1998–2004	Desperate Housewives ABC 2004–	Noah's Arc LOGO 2005–
"Urban"	"Suburban"	"Gay"
Miranda (Cynthia Nixon)	Lynette (Felicity Huffman)	Chance (Doug Spearman)
Carrie (Sarah Jessica Parker)	Susan (Teri Hatcher)	Alex (Rodney Chester)
Samantha (Kim Cattrall)	Gabrielle (Eva Longoria) & Edie (Nicollette Sheridan)	Ricky (Christian Vincent)
Charlotte (Kristin Davis)	Bree (Marcia Cross)	Noah (Darryl Stephens)

order to earn her diploma, while Blanche and Sophia compete for a suave Latin lover. Or Blanche and Rose try out for roles in *Cats* while Dorothy tries to prove that her mother is faking her injury. The permutations are many, and the laughs seem limitless.

Having popularized The Golden Rule of Four,[1] *The Golden Girls* is the thematic ancestor of many shows that followed, including some that still, subconsciously or consciously, employ it to this day. Only one year after *The Golden Girls*'s premiere, along came the Southern version (*Designing Women*), followed in the 1990s by the Black version (*Living Single*) and the urban (*Sex and the City*). In recent years, the formula has shown a resurgence in popularity, spawning a suburban version (*Desperate Housewives*) and, inevitably, the gay version (*Noah's Arc*).

Q FACT: In the fall of 2005, the WB network premiered a new hour-long series *Related*, which could be considered the "sibling" version of the formula. The show, which was created by *Sex and the City* alumna Liz Tuccillo, was cancelled after one eighteen-episode season by the new CW network in 2006.

[1] It's unclear whether we should credit the 1979–88 NBC sitcom *The Facts of Life* as a pre–*Golden Girls* inventor of the Rule of Four. Set at Peekskill, New York's fictional Eastland Academy, the show did not pare its large cast down to only four girls until its second season, beginning in 1980. And while Blair (Lisa Whelchel) can be considered a teenage Blanche, Natalie (Mindy Cohn) an outrageous and ethnic Sophia, and lesbian-icon Jo (Nancy McKeon) a tough-talking Dorothy, is Tootie (Kim Fields) really as naïve and dim-witted as Rose?

IN *DESIGNING WOMEN,* which launched in 1986, vain Southern beauty queen Suzanne Sugarbaker would certainly sense sisterhood with Blanche. And apart from the accent, Charlene Frazier's hometown of Poplar Bluff, Missouri, could easily be mistaken for Rose's birthplace, St. Olaf, Minnesota. Suzanne's older sister Julia Sugarbaker is clearly the Dorothy of the group—smart, opinionated, and prone to speak her mind, to the point of getting herself in trouble. Only Annie Potts's character of Mary Jo Shively is not easy to match up to a Golden Girl, perhaps because at the start, Mary Jo was the show's least defined character. Over the course of seven seasons, initially shy Mary Jo grew into her own and developed feminist ideals— and became a mini-Julia, another Dorothy. So it's no surprise that, after his initial appearance in an early first season episode (and also after, by the way, actor Meshach Taylor's small role in *The Golden Girls* pilot as a cop), *Designing Women* quickly promoted black delivery man Anthony Bouvier to regular status; like Sophia, he provides needed commentary on the often foolish actions of the women around him, and does so from an outsider's perspective, this time due to race and gender rather than age.

Starting in 1993 on FOX, *Living Single* was almost a direct copy of *The Golden Girls*, with its characters of Khadijah and Synclaire James and Regine Hunter fitting perfectly into the molds established by Dorothy, Rose, and Blanche, respectively. Again, only the Sophia role seems hard to fill, perhaps because when creating a show about young black women, there's no obvious parallel for an old lady. But Erika Alexander's character

Maxine Shaw comes pretty close; in her flirtatious banter with upstairs neighbor Kyle, she can be the most outrageous and outspoken of the four friends.

In HBO's hit—and gay favorite—*Sex and the City*, it's quite obvious which of the characters is "the slut" and which one is just a little bit naïve. And while both Miranda Hobbes and Carrie Bradshaw have moments of Dorothy-like cynicism, it's Miranda who is the true master of the form. Although not a perfect fit in the Sophia role, obviously younger and sexier Carrie does share some of the old woman's characteristics; in "diner scenes," the show's equivalent of "cheesecake scenes," Carrie, like Sophia, is often the character to go for the joke to sum up the situation, even at her friends' expense. And just as Sophia sums up her roommates' problems with pithy one-liners, Carrie literally narrates the travails of her friends, boiling them down to a weekly theme and typing it on her laptop screen.

Having tinkered with the formula in 1994 by creating the short-lived *The Five Mrs. Buchanans* for CBS, Marc Cherry found his greatest success ten years later with a show that owes a lot to the four ladies from Miami. "Blanche was my favorite character to write for," Marc remembers, "because the character was so selfish and vain and self-obsessed, and yet you still liked her." Comparing the earlier show to his current hit *Desperate Housewives*, Marc admits "there are a lot of traces of Blanche Devereaux in Gabrielle Solis. It's totally a credit to the actor. Like Rue McClanahan, Eva Longoria is one of those actors who is able to be likeable when she is doing some unlikable things."

Marc says that although his training comes from *The*

Golden Girls, the construction of *Desperate Housewives* is more akin to that of one of its younger siblings under the Golden Rule of Four, *Sex and the City*. Thus, his Lynette Schavo equals Miranda, Bree Van De Kamp is Charlotte, and lead character Susan Mayer is akin to lead character Carrie. In creating Susan, "I chose to make the romantic character the show's anchor instead of the common-sense one, as was done on *The Golden Girls*," Marc explains. "Susan Harris' paradigm was so successful—and indeed, Linda Bloodworth-Thomason copied it on *Designing Women*—that I just chose to emulate something else."

Finally, and inevitably, in 2005 came the gay take—well, the *literally* gay take—on the formula, LOGO's *Noah's Arc*. "I didn't set out to make a *Golden Girls*," says the show's creator, Patrik-Ian Polk. "But I did want to do a show about four black gay men, and so there are obvious parallels. Writing for a quartet allows you to have different character types. *The Golden Girls* is the classic show to have done that, and so it certainly doesn't hurt for me as a writer to have that as an example to draw from, and to try sometimes to imitate that style."

While *The Golden Girls* was a multi-camera sitcom about women, *Noah's Arc* is a single-camera, serialized drama about men, so the shows are stylistically different. Yet, Patrik says, "The parallels do pop up. There are times when we'll have a funnier scene coming up with the four guys together, and I'll say to them, 'Think of this as a real *Golden Girls*–type scene.' And they'll immediately get it." Ultimately, Patrik says, paying homage to the *Girls* is a happy inevitability—hence

Noah's Arc's "Which Golden Girl Are You" discussion, which had to be cut for time from one of the show's first season episodes (see below). "*The Golden Girls* is such a strong part of our culture," Patrik explains, "that it's impossible not to refer to it in some way."

Lost Scene from *Noah's Arc*

IN THE FIRST episode of *Noah's Arc*, entitled "My One Temptation," the boys sat down—over cheesecake—and played a common gay man's game, "Which Golden Girl Are You?" The following "lost scene," which had to be deleted from the episode due to time constraints but is included as an extra on the show's season 1 DVD, shows that to fans of both foursomes, the answers were rather obvious.

EDDIE
I left y'all a surprise in the fridge as a thank-you for helping with the move.

Noah digs in the fridge.

EDDIE (CONT'D)
I know how much y'all like those Golden Girls reruns. And they always eat cheesecake, so—

NOAH
(CUTTING THE CAKE) That is so sweet. Isn't it, Chance?
Chance smiles and kisses Eddie.
ALEX

Which Golden Girl am I?

NOAH
Sophia. Mama with the smart mouth.

ALEX
Noah, you're Rose.

NOAH
You tryin' to say I'm dumb?

ALEX
No, extra sweet.

RICKY
Which one am I?

ALL
Blanche.

CHANCE
Okay, that's enough. (TO EDDIE AND KENYA)
You two? Get out! You're gonna be late for baby ballet!
Out! Out!

NOAH, ALEX, RICKY
Dorothy.

Sharing Cheesecake with Rue McClanahan

Q QUOTE: Betty says that I always ate the cheesecake, but it's not true. I would actually put a bite of cheesecake on my fork and move it close to my mouth—then when the camera cut to someone else, I'd put it on a plate under my chair. By the time they'd cut back to me, I would pretend to be chewing.

IT WAS STATED from the very beginning that Blanche was more Southern than Blanche DuBois. But the accent in Atlanta where Blanche is from is very slight—hardly funny enough. So I decided to go with my instinct and make her a kind of phony. My mother had a cousin, Ina Pearl, who was from Southern Oklahoma like everybody else, but put on an accent that was part extreme Southern belle and part her idea of upper-class British. It was a remarkable accent and it was really, obviously hers alone. Nobody in the family knew where she got it from and although she didn't think she was being funny,

I always did. So I played Blanche the way I felt Blanche. She thought an accentuated Southern accent like Ina Pearl's would be sexy and strong and attractive to men. She wanted to be a Southern heroine, like Vivien Leigh. In fact, that's who I think she thought she was.

But as we rehearsed the pilot, Jay Sandrich said to me, "No, no—I don't want to hear a Southern accent." He said he wanted just to hear my regular Oklahoma accent, which he thought was Southern. Well, there's no arguing with the director. So I sort of did what he asked and used a modified sort-of-Southern accent. When I heard we got picked up for thirteen episodes, I worried about it for a couple of months. Finally, when we came back to shoot in July, I went to Paul Witt and Tony Thomas and said, "Okay, I know I'm not supposed to play it with a Southern accent, so I have an idea— I'll do a real Mae West." And they said, "What are you talking about? Of *course* Blanche has a Southern accent!" And I said WHEW! And was thrilled I got to play it the way I wanted to in the first place.

I needed to pick a voice that wasn't Rue that would work to help me create a character. You can't just do your regular voice, your regular walk, your regular beliefs, your regular anything if you're creating a character. For example, the Blanche walk came to me very quickly after the pilot. That's not my natural walk, but it is hers. And I don't think there's anyone else on

Earth who walks like Blanche. Movement is very important to me in developing a role, and I think Blanche's walk showed self-assurance and her always being on top of the situation. If she was at the Rusty Anchor or on a date, she felt it was irresistible and beguiling. The shoes were a big part of it, the sound they made. I always have to know what a character is going to wear, and once I discovered the walk, Blanche always wore those slingbacks.

As self-involved as she was, Blanche also had a sense of humor about herself, if the jokes were coming from the right place. It was a delightful thing for me to discover early on that Blanche would find Sophia adorable. It's really her fault that Blanche got to be known as a slut, but Blanche would forgive her because she'd had a stroke, and find everything she said funny and endearing. So if Sophia said something particularly nasty, I'd laugh like, "Aw, you cute little thing," and never took offense. It helped the jokes work, because it avoided a sour note of actual hurt feelings, and kept the audience with us.

Blanche also had a conservative side that was a lot unlike me: she could be homophobic, which I'm not, and for example she was grossed out by her daughter's artificial insemination, which I wouldn't have been at all—I had to act all that. Really, none of us is at all like our character—Betty probably the least of all, because she has nothing but brains. Estelle isn't at all pushy and vitriolic like Sophia—but they both were New York funny. And because Dorothy is probably the "straightest," least eccentric character, Bea is like her in that way. They both have a very funny take on people and are quick witted, not suffering fools gladly. But certainly Dorothy's failure in life is completely different from Bea's huge successes. And when people ask me if I'm like Blanche, my standard answer is, just look at the facts: Blanche is a man-crazy, glamorous, extremely sexy Southern belle from Atlanta. And I'm not from Atlanta.

In truth, I actually don't see Blanche as a slut at all. She actually had fewer dates than anybody if you go back and count—Sophia had more going on sexually than Blanche did. But Blanche talked a lot. I think that she was married to George for a long time, and she never got over him. She was always looking for a replacement—she was looking for love. She was also oversexed. I had a best girlfriend like that. They do go well together. I'm not oversexed, but I was looking for love, and I got myself into a lot of trouble that way. In fact, my upcoming memoir is titled *My First Five Husbands… And the Ones Who Got Away*. Maybe there is more similarity with Blanche than I've realized.

CHAPTER FIVE

The Gays and the Girls

"Yes, I think that gay people like *The Golden Girls* because it's a nontraditional family—that's part of it. But I think it's also the outrageousness of it. It's like a friend of mine once said, 'Why do gay people love opera? Because it's so much bigger than life.'"

–Bea Arthur

AS IN REAL LIFE, the Gays and older *Girls* have gone together from the start. In fact, one of the world's most famous gay men may have been *The Golden Girls*'s very first fan. One of the series' early directors, Jim Drake, remembers how in the summer of 1985, Betty White knew that her friend Rock Hudson did not have very much longer to live. Having recently gone public with his struggle with AIDS, Rock was in steeply declining health. But Betty knew something that would cheer him up. And so, with the producers' permission, she sent Rock advance copies of the first few episodes of her new series. And her hunch was right—he loved it.

Soon after the show's September 1985 premiere, the gay community was in group-love with the *Girls*. "What was fun was that on Saturday night, the gay bars would stop the music at nine o'clock when the show would come on," Betty remembers. "They'd all watch the show, and then at nine-thirty, they'd turn off the TV and start the dancing again." And Matthew Diamond, one of the series' directors in its later seasons, remembers sitting with the actresses as they discussed one particular way The Gays were paying tribute. "It was a Friday morning, the morning of the episode's taping," he remembers, "when the four ladies and I would meet for breakfast and go over the script. A night or two before had been Halloween, and one of the ladies—I don't remember which one—had gone down to Santa Monica Boulevard to the parade. Then she came in that morning and said, 'You know what the best costumes were? Us!' Four guys had dressed up like the four *Golden Girls*—someone short playing Estelle, someone tall as Bea, someone blonde as Betty—and she thought they looked pretty good. They all just thought it was the most charming thing, and so did I."

Q FACT: In celebration of the show's twentieth anniversary year, on November 11, 2005, Lifetime aired a marathon of *Golden Girls* episodes, and chose out gay comic Judy Gold as one of the two hosts to present bits of *Golden* shtik along the way. For tell-it-like-it-is comic Gold, *Golden* is a perfect fit. "On *The Golden Girls*, there are no holds barred, it is so honest," Judy explains. "The Girls say exactly what they think, and the Gays like it when people are who they say they are."

And well before *Noah's Arc*, references to *The Golden Girls* began popping up in other forms of pop—and gay—culture. In 1989, Randy Brenner, Rob Battan, Michel Horvatz, and Craig Smith formed a theater company, Charity Parody, and mounted their spoof production of the classic musical *West Side Story*, now retitled *West Hollywood Story*, in that city's Plummer Park. The parody show, authorized by *Story* creators Stephen Sondheim and Leonard Bernstein to play for two nights as a benefit for the Chris Brownlee AIDS Hospice, followed the original's storyline, but with a twist: now, instead of the Sharks and the Jets, the conflict in 1980s West Hollywood was between the "Straights" and the "Chics." And the show's famous, climactic rumble would now take place not on tough neighborhood streets but instead on the fourth level of the parking structure at the Beverly Center mall. That is, if the rumble can be scheduled at all; one of the show's big jokes involves the two gangs not being able to come up with a mutually convenient time to fight—because neither side, gay nor straight, is willing to miss a Saturday night episode of *The Golden Girls*.

Produced with full sets, costumes, and even a thirty-piece orchestra on stage, the show was a success, with hundreds of people from within both the gay community and the entertainment industry flocking to the tiny theater. "I showed up on the second day and there were three or four lines stretching down three blocks," Randy remembers. In subsequent years through the mid-1990s, the company put on AIDS-benefit spoofs of *Gypsy*, *Fiddler on the Roof*, and *Oliver!*, each with at least one of the ladies—and always Estelle Getty—in attendance. And each time, there was at least one obligatory reference to those ladies from Miami. "We always made a list of things we knew had to be in the show, and *The Golden Girls* was always on the list," Randy explains. "Because the response to those references was always hooting, hollering, screaming, and laughing. It was great."

In 2003, theater duo and real-life couple Peter Mac and John Schaefer created a stage show that honored the series more directly. With two gay male friends joining them as Rose and Blanche, Peter and John appeared as Sophia and Dorothy in *Golden Girls... Live*, their all-drag version of the sitcom that sold out its limited four-show run and eventually played sixty performances at cabaret room Rose's Turn in New York's West Village.

Due to rights issues with the source material, their larger plans—including a new Dorothy/Sophia musical entitled "Shady Pines, Ma!"—never materialized. But for the Golden summer of 2003, gays and their fellow New Yorkers could enjoy a 3-D slice of their favorite cheesecake from Miami.

Why We Love Them

WHAT IS IT about these four older women that has now captivated several generations of gay men? Betty White has a theory, sort of: "I think that for some reason, gay men just like old ladies. I don't know why, but they do." Marc Cherry agrees, "Gay men appreciate women of a certain age." So do gay men and women like *The Golden Girls*, then, because, more than their straight counterparts, they respect aged wisdom, and value old ladies? Or is it because conversely, gay men and women sense that these particular four old ladies respect and value them?

1. Because They Love Us

For gay people who may not have perfect, accepting relationships with their own mothers and grandmothers, it certainly feels good to hear positive, liberal thinking about homosexuality come out of the mouths of sixty- and eighty-something women. When Dorothy shows that her friend Jean's lesbianism is no big deal to her, or Blanche learns to accept her gay brother Clayton, it gives us all hope. After all, if these grandmother figures on TV can learn to accept us, there's hope that our real family elders may ultimately do so, too.

The Girls' acceptance of gay life and gay rights extended beyond the TV tube as well, as the actresses were often politically active in real life, supporting gay causes. Having befriended many gay men during her days in the theater and in *Torch Song Trilogy* in particular, Estelle Getty was most comfortable when surrounded by, as her gay former assistant Richard Weaver remembers her jokingly calling it, "her five-fag minimum." And when those friends, and her own nephew, started to get sick, Estelle became one of Hollywood's first and most tireless celebrity AIDS activists and fundraisers. As recently as November 2005, Bea Arthur reprised her one-woman show, *Bea Arthur: Back on Broadway*, as a one-night engagement in New York benefiting the Ali Forney Center, a charity providing emergency housing for LGBT youth. And over the years, all four of the actresses have popped up in various AIDS-benefit performances or GLAAD Media Awards ceremonies, supporting that part of their fan base that so vocally supports them.

2. Because *They* Are *Us*

In truth, even if it weren't for their support of the gay community, the Girls would still be easy for gay people to love, because they remind us of some of the gay stereotypes we love to use to define ourselves—but hate when straight people use them to pigeonhole us. There's The Bitchy Queen (Dorothy), The Dizzy Queen (Rose), and everyone's favorite, The Slut (Blanche). Among ourselves, we even like to play with these roles as if they're a parlor game: "Which Golden Girl are you?" Every gay fan has already pondered this, and is ready with his or her answer.

3. Because They Take On Things That Scare or Threaten Us

Part of the show's overall brilliance was the way it tackled taboo topics, yet still managed to wring tremendous laughs out of the things that scared us most. *The Golden Girls* got to have its cheesecake and eat it too—and its secret weapon turned out to be the thing that today would be considered a disadvantage: the age of its characters. For some reason, audiences were more comfortable, or just more forgiving, hearing controversial, dark, or just plain outrageous words coming out of the mouths of older women. Especially older women like stroke-addled Sophia, who at least had an excuse. And so, where other shows might not have had as wide a berth with the network or the viewing public, the Girls were given license to slip us some life lessons along with the laughs. Over the years, they addressed ageism, immigration, homelessness, and the lack of affordable healthcare. But gay viewers particularly appreciated the way the show, on numerous occasions, took on homosexuality and AIDS, all the while providing an outlet to laugh and take a break from the seriousness and sadness of it all.

4. Because They Love Each Other

The roommates at 5161 Richmond Street are 100 percent "out" about loving each other, even if they do mean it in a purely platonic way. In their house, loving a friend is viewed as something completely natural, to be expressed openly, not to be nervous about. As the Girls see it, it's only polite, and completely reasonable, for them to double, even triple up in a bed so as to house

BEING A FRIEND:
A CONVERSATION WITH
JOHN SCHAEFER AND
PETER MAC

PETER MAC is a singer, actor, and female impressionist. With a doctorate degree in information technology, John Schaefer is a Wall Street computer consultant by day, "male actress" by night. Real-life boyfriends who met at a *Wizard of Oz*–themed brunch in Chelsea— does it get any gayer than that?—they cooked up the idea for stage show *Golden Girls... Live* one morning over breakfast and turned it into a benefit to fight progressive supranuclear palsy, the disease with which Estelle Getty had been at the time diagnosed. (The diagnosis was later changed to Lewy Body Dementia.) The shorter—although younger—of the two, Peter had a knack for Sophia's mannerisms, while John reluctantly took on the role of Dorothy and turned out to be a natural at capturing Bea Arthur's trademark slow burn.

PETER: I was rehearsing a play I had written called *Judy and Me* when all of a sudden someone said "lesbian." And someone else said, à la Blanche, "*les*bian." Within minutes, we were quoting an entire episode of the show. And I realized it's a rite of passage for gay men to know every single line of this TV series. John and I had just started dating, and I discovered that he had had the same idea—wouldn't it be great if four guys dressed up and did the show live on stage? Because Estelle did so much charity work to fight AIDS, we did those shows as a benefit to fight her disease, as a nice payback to help her. We pulled together a cast—my friend Darren Polito played Blanche. He's a very short, Italian gentleman—looks nothing like Rue. But he's got all of her mannerisms down flawlessly. Several gay friends played Rose at different times during the run. We got all our costumes on eBay, including that very distinct wicker purse, which had to be just right.

JOHN: Immediately, the show took on a life of its own. We got lots of press right away, including in *People* and *Entertainment Weekly*, and our first four shows sold out as soon as they were listed in the local gay magazines. The phone rang off the hook and drove the bartenders crazy. They had to turn away people who had lined up around the block, and there was a long waiting list.

I had never performed as Bea Arthur, and Peter had had to convince me to play Dorothy. It was a little weird being boyfriends playing mother and daughter, although Michael Musto wrote in his *Village Voice* column that that made him hot. Plus, I always thought Sophia had the better lines. Peter had to convince me that

Dorothy was the "star." And after all, I love Bea Arthur. I already knew a lot of her mannerisms from repeated viewings of the movie *Mame*. Ironically, now I still play her in *Judy and Bea*, the cabaret show Peter and I perform at Helen's in Chelsea.

PETER: John and I are both half-Italian, and that may be why we both liked Sophia so much. She was my aunts Josie and Adeline and my grandmother all combined into one—these little Italian women you didn't want to cross.

Our audience was usually at least sixty percent gay men—a fun, strange cross-section of leather daddies, bachelorette, and birthday parties and sorority groups. When the lights went down and the theme song started to play, everybody would sing along. And once we entered in costume, it would take a few minutes to calm them down. It was a lot like "Rocky Horror," because they would say the lines with us on some nights. People had fun being so close to the "Girls" who weren't trapped in that little box anymore.

We performed two episodes—"Break In," from the first season, where after a robbery Rose is traumatized and buys a gun, and Sophia has some of her best lines. And then it seemed fitting that the other one should be the lesbian episode, "Isn't It Romantic," from season two. We did them word for word, inflection for inflection, which is important, because the audience knows the show so well. And in between, Sophia would come out and interact with the audience, which is really when I could have fun with it, because Sophia is one of the few TV characters who can get away with saying anything, all while running a *Golden Girls* trivia contest and passing out cheesecake.

JOHN: These people were drinking, so occasionally, we'd get heckled. One night, when Sophia insulted a gay guy in the front row during intermission, he growled, "Don't start with me, bitch!" And so Dorothy came out to save Ma. I said, "You're going to have to deal with me, mister. And I warn you, I did time in Attica." And then Peter said, "Isn't Attica a *men's* prison?" The actual lines from the show made for great ammo.

We know the Girls were aware of our show—Betty even mentioned it when she appeared on Ellen DeGeneres' talk show. It was important to us that they and the audience knew that we were doing the show as a tribute, in a loving way. We were having fun with it, not making fun. And we definitely struck a chord with people. One night after a show I came downstairs for a drink, and the glass slipped, hit the bar, and cut my hand open. We went to St. Vincent's Hospital and got carte blanche treatment. Or carte Blanche, as it were. Every nurse in triage was coming in to see "The Golden Girls."

a visiting relative comfortably. On their lanai, Girl-on-Girl hugs and group huddles are everyday occurrences. In fact, no one thinks twice about touching a member of the same sex—that is, until the show cleverly decides to have it both ways. Because you can be sure that when Blanche and Rose rehearse their "Dirty Dancing" routine, or Blanche decides to demonstrate on Dorothy the ear-blowing technique that drives men wild, Sophia will enter the room on cue, to witness it all with a "well, well, look at the lesbians" wisecrack. And for gay members of the audience who remember too well the closeted days when one dared not get caught touching a same-sex "friend," Sophia's jokes provide much-appreciated laughter and release.

5. Because They Love Men

And so do we. And they sure get plenty of them. Through the Girls, we get to live in the fantasy that suitors are and always will be in great supply, even when we're older.

6. Because They've Been Through What We've Been Through

Among the four Girls, only divorcee Dorothy had a man who is still alive (not that she's always thrilled about that). As widows, Blanche, Rose, and Sophia know what it was like to lose the men they loved. And so, for fans—especially gay men who, over the years, have lost friends and lovers to AIDS—the Girls provide inspiration that despite such tragic loss, you can survive, and even thrive, with a little help from your friends.

7. Because Through It All, They Choose Each Other

Kids and grandkids may pop in and out, but it's clear to us that the four Girls themselves are the true family unit. With only two of them actually related by blood, they're not lower-case "family" in the literal, Republican sense of the word, but more unconventional "Family." It's no accident that gay men and women use the same word as code to identify each other; it's important to us to surround ourselves with people who understand and support us. Just as we often build surrogate families out of our friends, the Girls choose to be together, even to the point of eschewing contact with their biological relatives. Instead of hanging out with kids who would treat them like helpless old ladies, they've built the fantasy Family we all yearn for. And so, when a freak snowstorm or a gun-toting Santa forces the Girls to forego flights "home" and instead spend Christmas together, we're happier because we know the Girls are truly happier that way, too.

8. Because We Love (and Love to Hate) Their Style

Whether you loved or loved to hate their wardrobes, you have to admit that the Girls' must have been the most stylin' house on all of Richmond Street. As anyone who has ever visited Nana in her nursing home knows, "women of a certain age" are not always so immaculately made-up and coiffed as Dorothy, Blanche and Rose—even eighty-something Sophia, whose white curls stayed forever as crisp as her spaghetti *al dente*. And whether you think them fashion-forward or fashion victims, any gay fan has got to give the ladies their props for obviously spending their entire social security checks, and then some, following '80s and '90s trends and commissioning custom couture.

Judy Evans Steele, the show's costume designer, reports that during the show's run, she regularly received fan mail from viewers wanting to know where she got Dorothy's vest or Blanche's skirt. (And, not wanting to break their hearts with news that the items were not available in stores, she often enclosed a photocopy of her design sketch and a swatch of fabric along with her reply.) As the '80s continue to make a comeback on designer runways, Judy's original designs have the power to divide us into two camps even today. Designer Zulema Griffin admires Dorothy's wardrobe, full of cowl-neck, oversized tops, wide-leg Capri bottoms, and slouchy boots, a style which she calls "unique and flattering to tall women." *Noah's Arc* actor Doug Spearman agrees: "My number one fashion choice was the year or two when Dorothy adopted the white suede, low-heeled boots. She wore them with everything. Very elfish, very pre–*Lord of the Rings*. I adored those boots. I covet those boots." And although designer John Bartlett calls Dorothy's style "beyond freaky," he does appreciate Blanche's taste in Florida daywear.

But as detractors are just as quick to point out: what the hell was with that bride-from-Mars, white-toilet-paper-roll wedding dress, Dorothy?

9. *Because They Love a Good Showtune*

While it's true that "Miami, You've Got Style" is no "New York, New York," Dorothy still sings the homemade ode to their Florida hometown better than your average substitute schoolteacher should. From the dawn of gay time, we've gone simply mad for a smart-talking dame who can belt out a showtune, as Dorothy does in the Rusty Anchor. Or tap dance through the living room like Rose and Blanche—all while showing some pretty glam gams for gals getting up there in age. Whether it's Rose showing her mastery of the piano (something which Betty, by the way, has to fake) or the three ladies busting some choreographed moves during a lullaby of "Mr. Sandman," these grannies show that they've got it all. They can sing, they can dance, *and* tell jokes? What's not for a gay fan to love?

10. Because... They're Funny!

Make that hysterically funny. These four Girls toss around the witty, sometimes bitchy banter gay men and women love. They deliver the fantasy put-downs we wish we could and looking back, wish we had. For example, in the fourth season episode, "Yes, We Have No Havanas," when Sophia and Blanche are competing for the attention of Latin lover Fidel, Blanche sashays her way through the living room announcing her intention of taking a steamy bath, with just enough water to cover her bosoms. Sophia's response: "You're only gonna sit in an inch of water?"

Now who doesn't wish he or she had said that?!

Such Gay Repartee from the Straight Man

Q QUOTE: *"When you're around a rewrite table, 90 percent of the time you wander off-story, just laughing with each other about something. You make fun of each other, and everyone is fair game. Any time I hire anyone, I make it clear that their sexual mores, religious beliefs, and all ideas about life itself are all going to be challenged, because some of the people in that room are brilliantly funny. And I'm not going to stop people from being funny just because you don't want to hear a joke about Jesus. But running a table can be a tricky thing. I remember one night in particular where a couple of writers had stepped over the line. It became like gay bashing, and I had to step in and stop it. Later on, I called Marc and Jamie at home and apologized for not having done so sooner."—Marc Sotkin*

From the very beginning of its six years on the air, viewers of *Sex and the City* often noted that, with their obsessions with all things sexual, the show's four heroines actually sounded a whole lot more like gay men in dresses. From some this was a criticism, from others, a compliment. Either way, the same could be said—and has been—about *Sex and the City*'s predecessor, *The Golden Girls*. In the case of the HBO hit, the "they're really gay men" theory has an understandable origin: the show was created by an out gay man, Darren Star, and produced throughout its run by out gay showrunner Michael Patrick King and a small staff of women and gay men. But with *The Golden Girls*, this was surprisingly not the case.

"As a gay man watching the show, I just assumed it was going to be just the biggest old group of gay guys writing it," says Marc Cherry, who joined the *Golden Girls* staff in the show's fifth season. "And then the most astonishing thing was—it wasn't." As he and then-writing partner Jamie Wooten became only the *Girls'* second out writing team, and the only gay people writing on the show at that time, Marc realized that fitting in might turn out to be a bigger challenge than he had anticipated. "The very first day around lunchtime, everyone started talking about their favorite boxing matches. And I was so depressed, because I thought, 'These people can't be doing this!'" But Marc soon came to be impressed with how well the show's straight, mostly male writing staff was able to channel their inner Golden Girls—and how well they deployed one of their secret weapons. "The four Girls would make the dirtiest jokes—we actually had an in-joke in the scripts: we'd write in the stage directions, 'And then they laughed like men!'" he remembers. "These were conversations we hoped our grandmothers weren't having. But the fascinating thing was, gay or straight, you would just write what you thought was a really great joke—and then you would put it in Bea Arthur's

BEHIND THE SCENES: A CONVERSATION WITH STAN ZIMMERMAN AND JAMES BERG

WE STARTED writing together after we met at NYU. After graduating, we wrote a few sample scripts and then worked on an ABC sitcom that lasted only thirteen episodes. We were very young and we got very lucky—we got the chance to come in and pitch a freelance episode to *The Golden Girls* in its first season.

Well, we pitched a few ideas, and the producers didn't like any of them. We realized as we were in the doorway about to leave, "Oh fuck—we haven't sold anything!" So we threw out a sentence about Rose's mother visiting, and luckily, they loved it. They hired us to write the script, and when they loved that, too, they brought us on staff.

We were breaking ground not only as young writers but as gay writers, because a gay writing team was unheard of at the time. Agents and other people in the business advised us not to tell people we were gay, and if there were industry events to go to, we should bring a woman as a beard. Back in those days, TV writing staffs were all straight-guy clubs. When we first got to LA, we heard that on Garry Marshall's shows, they played basketball in-between writing, and we thought, "We're never going to make it." And when we were on the show before *Golden Girls*, one of us came in one Monday and mentioned having been to an AIDS-benefit garage sale, and the writers freaked out and said to throw out the clothes or we would end up getting sick. That was the mentality at the time.

But as much as we wanted to fit in, we didn't lie. We just didn't ever bring up the gay aspect of our lives. But that's hard, when you spend that many hours a day with people—now we can't even imagine doing that. Of course, if we got friendly with any of the writers, the truth would end up coming out. And from her years in the theater, Estelle recognized us as gay immediately—it was like we had a secret code. She asked us outright, and we were like, "How did you know?!" She told us she wanted to take us out and introduce us around, and we ended up becoming very close with her.

Marc Cherry has been very sweet about acknowledging our paving the way for out gay writers on *The Golden Girls*. The whole thing is ironic, because it was always a show that had a gay sensibility to it, even if it wasn't always spoken about. It had a bitchy, witty quality, and was about women who, like gay men, had been through a lot. They all had sex without it being a big deal. They lost their families and had to create new ones when they moved away. It all had so much in common with gay culture. And maybe it's because we're gay men, we found out we were particularly good at writing for not only these old women, but women in general.

After our year on *The Golden Girls*, we were meeting in 1986 for a job on the sitcom version of the movie *Gung Ho*, and the executive asked, "You're lavenders, aren't you?" The two of us looked at each other and gasped as if the air had been sucked from the room. Here's this man not only saying that we're gay, but he's using some kind of new word for it! Not just "friends of Dorothy," but now "lavenders"? We both went immediately to the purple/gay thing. Well, it turns out, the Lavenders are NYU's team. We didn't even know they had a sports team.

Eventually, of course, things changed. We were among the first writers to come out publicly, when we were featured in an article about "out" writers in Hollywood in *LA Weekly* magazine. When we worked on *Roseanne*, Tom Arnold called us his gay guys, and requested us to work on scripts. And although we weren't out to Mort Nathan and Barry Fanaro when we worked for them on *The Golden Girls*, we all worked together on a pilot years later and were able to joke about the whole thing. One of them would hold up a magazine with the picture of a supermodel centerfold and would ask, "Nothing? You feel nothing?" They teasingly acted like they just couldn't grasp that. So then we would hold up a gay magazine with some handsome guy with his shirt off, and ask them the same question.

mouth and it would come out gay."

Jamie Wooten also remembers that, after having assumed *The Golden Girls* staff would be like a gay family reunion, he found himself wondering how to break into an established clique of "manly men." The writing process on the show was, Jamie remembers, "Some kind of weird alchemy. The writers wrote the characters like they were men, and then the women got a hold of it and it would magically work. And the audience just thought these women were so brilliantly honest and original, because this is the kind of stuff you hardly ever heard coming out of women's mouths."

Keep It Light, Keep It Bright, Keep It Gay

Stan Zimmerman and James Berg, a writing team from the show's first season, do think that being gay was an asset for two young men trying to capture four older ladies' voices. "We found that as gay men, we liked writing for women. Whether it is old women or teenage girls, we realized we have their voices," James says. "And since then," Stan adds, "our career has really been about writing for women. We have been known for having that voice."

But incredibly, four years later, being gay almost cost Marc and Jamie, authors of arguably some of *The Golden Girls*'s greatest later-season episodes, their shot at writing for the show at all. When they first started on the show, the two starving writers were roommates as well. As they were hired to write their first freelance episode, they submitted their paperwork to the studio's business affairs department, and their common address triggered an alarm: are they boyfriends? A lower-level producer brought the situation to the attention of executive producer Marc Sotkin. "He said something along the lines of, 'Do we really want to hire two gay lovers?' And Marc looked at him and said, 'I am not even going to entertain that as a question,'" Marc Cherry explains. "So let me just say my whole career is probably based on that one decision, and on Marc Sotkin being a stand-up guy. And the joke was, Jamie and I weren't lovers, and never had been."

Eventually, Marc says, his fellow writers came to see that having a gay man or two around on staff could sometimes be an asset. In one circumstance, Marc Sotkin called on Marc and Jamie to convince the straight male network censor that a particular gay joke in the script was not offensive to gay men. (They lost, and had to change the words "gay man" to "drag queen." See episode #138: "Girls Just Wanna Have Fun… Before They Die.") And as Jamie remembers, in season seven, when the duo wrote Rue McClanahan's favorite episode, "Journey to the Center of Attention," they also got to pick all the songs that both Dorothy and Blanche perform at the Rusty Anchor bar. Bea loved their choices for Dorothy, "Hard-Hearted Hannah" and "What'll I Do." And for Blanche, there was "I Wanna Be Loved By You," which Rue performed so memorably, awkwardly losing control of the microphone and ultimately her balance as she attempted to vamp atop a piano à la Michelle Pfeiffer in *The Fabulous Baker Boys*. "Again, the gay thing was an asset," Jamie remembers. "The other people on staff didn't know or care that Bea

Arthur had ever been a Broadway star or could sing. So Marc and I made sure to write that opportunity for her, and made sure she had two songs."

But it turns out, that's not exactly true—just a nasty generalization of straight people based on a stereotype. For example, Jim Vallely, one of the show's straight writers who is, by all accounts, responsible for some of its greatest one-liners, admits to having had an unnatural childhood obsession with Bea Arthur singing "Bosom Buddies" in the movie *Mame*. That's right—the Lucy version. Enough said.

CELEBRITY SURVEY #3: WHICH OF THE GIRLS IS YOUR FAVORITE?

DOROTHY. I love her takes—those long, very dry looks she gave the others, especially Rose.

—Ben Patrick Johnson, author of *Third and Heaven*

BLANCHE. Because as much as I identify with Dorothy, I'd rather be Blanche.

—Doug Spearman, actor

ROSE. I wanted Betty White to be my mother. She looked like my mother—but was less vague about reality.

—Tom Bianchi, artist/author

SOPHIA. I base the success of each episode on how funny she was.

—Craig Chester, actor/writer/director of *Adam & Steve*

SOPHIA. She typically was the most interesting character and, from a writer's standpoint, it's got to be a joy to write for someone who's had a stroke and can, therefore, say anything for any reason. What a dream!

—Billy Masters, syndicated columnist and performer

ROSE. Because she's the smartest idiot of them all. And she consistently has better hair. Very important.

—Ted Casablanca, E! Online Gossip Guru and columnist of "The Awful Truth"

DOROTHY. I've been a huge Bea Arthur fan my whole life, since her *Maude* days. Her slow burns to the camera are priceless. That woman's got comic timing to die for.

—Dan Bucatinsky, actor/writer/producer

BLANCHE. Because she's living out the life I secretly wish I had. She to me is the sexual revolution embodied as a human being. I wish I could be as emboldened as she is.

—ANT, stand-up comedian and host of VH1's *Celebrity Fit Club*

DOROTHY. I love an underdog. You can see the exact reason for the failure in her love life in her mother, and yet she has dedicated a good portion of her post-marriage life to taking care of her. She wins after all.

—Jermaine Taylor, panelist, GSN's *I've Got a Secret*

ROSE. I love her simplicity and how over the years you got to see how smart and how competitive she was.

—Bruce Daniels, comic

SOPHIA, of course. She calls 'em as she sees 'em, even if she doesn't see 'em too clearly.
 –Bruce Vilanch, writer/performer

BLANCHE, because she shows how the force of your own confidence and charm can make you even more attractive than whatever looks nature has bestowed upon you.
 –Dan Mathews, vice president of People for the Ethical Treatment of Animals (PETA)

ROSE. She is so sweet and a bit thick, but always has her heart in the right place. And I love her endless and nonsensical stories about home.
 –John Bartlett, designer

DOROTHY. But I love them all because they are so honest and committed, but the fact that they're so mean to each other is the greatest thing in the world. They are like a bunch of nasty queens.
 –Judy Gold, actress/writer/stand-up comedian

ROSE. She always seems so hapless, and then she surprises you with a sudden understanding of the world around her. The writers always gave her the best stuff to work with.
 –Derek Hartley, talk show host, Sirius Satellite Radio

SOPHIA. I think she's just a wise old sage and she says what everyone else is thinking.
    —Dennis Hensley, "Twist" radio host and author of *Misadventures in the (213)*

SOPHIA. I just love that she just says whatever the hell she feels like saying. I aspire to that freedom and lack of inhibition. How liberating it must be to not ever care about tact.
    —Rex Lee, actor, HBO's *Entourage*

DOROTHY, mainly because I am a huge Bea Arthur fan. There is nothing more brilliant than a slow Bea Arthur head take! Her turn and glare is unmatched!
    —Varla Jean Merman, cabaret performer and actress, *Girls Will Be Girls*

ROSE. First of all, I'm Swedish like she is. And who does not love Betty White?
    —Mark Lund, television personality

SOPHIA. She always reminds me of my grandmother who was short, white-haired, carried a pocketbook at all times, and always said exactly what was on her mind without ever worrying that she might offend. After she died, Sophia became my surrogate TV Nana.
    —Frank DeCaro, talk show host, Sirius Satellite Radio, and panelist on GSN's *I've Got a Secret*

ROSE. I love Betty White and I love the character. She's the wacky, silly person who actually has it all figured out.

—Robert Verdi, stylist, actor, and host of Discovery Channel's *Surprise By Design*

This is the obvious question, but one that is so hard to answer. Because every time you think it's one gal, you think about the other ones and realize how much you love them too.

—Ari Gold, musician and DJ

WHICH OF THE GIRLS IS *YOUR* FAVORITE?

CHAPTER SIX

Q-Friendly Episodes

STARTING WITH *The Mary Tyler Moore Show* in the early 1970s, it has not been unusual for any halfway-decent, liberal-minded sitcom to produce "The Gay Episode." The format, which became increasingly popular in the '80s, is often the same: a long-lost friend of one of the show's regulars comes to town, stunning his or her host with a declaration of alternative sexuality. Twenty or so minutes later, all is forgiven, all are enlightened—and we never hear from the visiting homo again. *Mary* got a visit from Phyllis Lindstrom's brother. *Cheers'* Sam Malone heard from a former baseball teammate, and *Designing Women's* Suzanne Sugarbaker from a former beauty pageant rival. *Dear John's* John Lacey finds out that a pal from the past is in love with him. And George, of *The Jeffersons*, gets the biggest shock of all: his old Navy buddy is now a woman. But *The Golden Girls* broke new ground, bringing LGBT characters and storylines into American living rooms not just once, but many times during each of its seven seasons on the air. This section highlights the *Golden* episodes overtly touching on gay, lesbian, and transgender issues, as well as those that just pique our interest with a campy moment or a hunky guest.

Season 1, Episode 1: "Pilot"

WRITTEN BY: Susan Harris

DIRECTED BY: Jay Sandrich

ORIGINAL AIR DATE: September 14, 1985

SYNOPSIS: Blanche has been dating Harry, a man whom the other women suspect she will eventually marry. Their suspicions are confirmed when Blanche comes home from a date with Harry, all aflutter with marriage plans. Rose and Dorothy realize that Blanche's forthcoming union will mean a change of address for them. And worse yet, as the day of the wedding dawns, Rose is struck with a sinking feeling about Harry. She wants to tell Blanche of her doubts, but Dorothy prevents her from doing so. Then, while they all wait for Harry to arrive for the ceremony, a policeman arrives at the house to tell Blanche that she has become involved with a bigamist, sending Blanche reeling into a deep depression. The other women attempt, and fail, to cheer her up. But eventually, Blanche does emerge from her bedroom, renewed with the realization that she would be hard-pressed to find the love and support from someone else that she has found with her roommates and friends.

COMMENTARY: Trivia buffs take note: this episode marks the sole appearance of the Girls' gay houseboy, Coco. But after heavy editing of the pilot for time, not much remains of Charles Levin's original performance. His presence remains the strongest in the show's opening scene, which introduces Dorothy Zbornak as she comes home from a hard day of substitute teaching, complaining about the hoodlums in her class. After all, with her roommates Blanche and Rose not having been introduced yet, and Shady Pines not yet having burned down, who else would Dorothy have to communicate her precious plot exposition to if not for Coco?

The episode also features future *Designing Women* regular Meshach Taylor in a small role as the policeman.

SUSAN HARRIS: In a pilot, you have so many problems to solve in such a short amount of time, there's just so much you can do. You just hope to establish characters, their back story, and the story that you're about to tell. That's all you've got room for in your twenty-three minutes and change.

MITCH HURWITZ: The thing that Susan can't say, so I will, is that it is so brilliantly written. The characters are well formed. As a template for the future, it's all there. It all crystallizes at this moment.

MARC CHERRY: The thing I'm really impressed with in the pilot is how subtly and gracefully Susan gets the plot exposition out. When Rose says about Blanche, "She'll lose her job at the museum!" as a writer you think, "Look at that—now we know what Blanche does."

PAUL WITT: When you're hoping that all the right talent comes together at just the right time, there's always an element of luck when you make a pilot. But we knew we had a great piece of material. Susan's script is widely considered one of the best pilots ever written. And thanks to our amazing cast, it turned out to be one of the best pilots made.

Campy Guest Star Alert:

Season 1, Episode #23: Polly Holliday as Lilly Lindstrom in "Blind Ambitions"

ORIGINAL AIR DATE: March 29, 1986

SIX YEARS AFTER she last told her boss Mel Sharples to kiss her grits on CBS sitcom *Alice*, Polly Holliday has left Phoenix and arrived in Miami, albeit a little less independent as Lilly Lindstrom, Rose's newly blind sister. But she gets a taste of her own sassy grits when Rose stops coddling her and shows her some tough love, forcing her to learn to get along on her own.

Campy Guest Star Alert:

Season 1, Episode #24: Peggy Pope in "Big Daddy"

ORIGINAL AIR DATE: May 23, 1986

AS IN HER TRADEMARK ROLE in the feature film *9 to 5*, here Peggy Pope takes the supporting part of neighbor Gladys Barton and adds her patented, slurring *je ne sais quoi*—to which we've gotta salute her with an "Attagirl!" And in another gay history crossover, this episode also features Gary Grubbs, who was initially

BEING A FRIEND: A CONVERSATION WITH CHARLES LEVIN

I HAD NO concern whatsoever about playing a gay character. I grew up in the theater, and played all different parts, heterosexual and homosexual. The '80s were a more innocent time, a time of coming out. But they were also still a time of lisping, effeminate gay characters on TV. My physical type doesn't lend itself well to that stereotype, but what I could do was affect it.

Unlike my *Hill Street Blues* character Eddie Gregg, whose life ended heroically but tragically, Coco was a gay character being played for laughs. Susan Harris has a great track record of doing that, like with Billy Crystal on *Soap*. The way she wrote Coco, he was obviously gay and loving it. Even though he was way over the top, this was a real person, and you're allowed to laugh and enjoy him without feeling self-conscious or afraid that he's gay. And he was completely acceptable to all the women in the house—that was the irony of the title, that he, too, was a "Golden Girl."

I think including a gay character in the show was a stroke of brilliance, because Coco lent an air of authenticity. Even back then, Miami was getting more flamboyant and body-beautiful all the time, and had a thriving gay population without making a big deal about it. Coco reflected the reality of the locale, which TV mostly doesn't care about, especially in sitcoms.

Susan wanted to write a character who gave you insights as to what gay guys do—their love lives, their private lives. But as I found out during rehearsal week, that was verboten. I had a scene where I come in and announce, "That's the last time I date a cop!" I pour my heart out to Sophia, my confidante, and she decides to cheer me up by taking me to the dog track. Well, word came down that this was offensive to NBC, who did not want any reference to what Coco was doing with other men. The scene was cut. Nobody wanted to know what he did on the outside. His only function was to be within the house, dealing with the women. I think one of the real problems was that Rock Hudson was dying of AIDS. I think it threw everyone for a loop, especially those in TV. Because now, how do you deal with gay characters when there's this threat of a horrible death hanging over their heads? So any mention of intercourse between men was just not going to be tolerated—it was too frightening.

The night of the taping, I went home on cloud nine. Over the next few weeks, as I waited for the official pickup of my "option," my wife and I were getting calls about when the limo would be picking us up for the network affiliates meeting, and what to wear. And then, two days before the option deadline, Paul Witt called and said, "Chuck, it's not going to work out." He explained that there were too many people in the show, and that they really wanted to concentrate on the women. They didn't want to have to give me less to do just to keep me in the show—it wouldn't be fair to me.

I was devastated, simply because it was such a great show. I didn't care about the money—that stuff has never been important to me. But I'd fallen in love with Bea and Estelle. I've actually never seen the pilot as it ended up airing. I refused to watch it because I remember what it was, and it's too disappointing to see how it was butchered. Basically what you see now is that I'm sort of a walk-through.

Unfortunately, when you're released from a hit show or pilot, I guess word gets around. And so this made me a pariah for almost two years. It really wasn't until I played a *mohel* on *Seinfeld* years later that I got "rediscovered." That's the role I'm recognized most for, or sometimes Eddie Gregg—never Coco.

Of the three memorable characters I've played in my career, two of them have been gay, and I'm proud of that. My wife Kathy and I both grew up in the theater, and our best friends were gay. Our daughter is gay, as is my closest nephew, who is like my third son. We're part of a gay-straight ministry at our church in Orange County, California, called EFLAGS, and now we're starting other chapters around the country within the Episcopal church. I still think back on my *Golden Girls* experience fondly, and don't have any regrets. I just sometimes grieve the loss of that character, who could have grown into something wonderful.

a regular on *Will & Grace*, the first sitcom to be created with a gay character as one of its leads. But as happens on TV, Grubbs's *W&G* character, Will's prime client Harlin Polk, survived only half of the show's first season before being written out.

Season 2, Episode #26, "The End of the Curse"

WRITTEN BY: Susan Harris
DIRECTED BY: Terry Hughes
ORIGINAL AIR DATE: September 27, 1986
SYNOPSIS: Blanche is startled to discover that, having lost track of her cycle, she may be pregnant. But when the doctor's diagnosis is not pregnancy but instead the onset of menopause, Blanche goes into a deep depression and refuses to leave her room. Meanwhile, the other three ladies decide to breed minks for profit. Their efforts are thwarted, however, when the minks fail to show any interest in each other. Rose sets up a vigil, despite Sophia declaring she is "sick" for monitoring their behavior. Dorothy and the ladies drag Blanche to a psychiatrist to deal with her depression about menopause. But the cure

for her depression, not surprisingly, comes instead in the form of a handsome veterinarian who arrives to check on the minks. When he tells the ladies the minks are too old to breed, Blanche decides to question him on other "animal" matters in private. Rose convinces the ladies that the minks are not useless just because they are too old, and Blanche wholeheartedly agrees: the minks stay. And just as the decision is made, two of the minks do start to get frisky after all. The problem is, they're both males.

COMMENTARY: Gay minks! Actually, the alternative lifestyle of the minks may be the only aspect of this episode's "B" plot that Bea Arthur, Rue McClanahan, and Betty White found at all amusing. All three of them animal activists, the ladies hated doing an episode showing the Girls farming animals for fur, but all agree that it was too late in the process to refuse to do the script, lest they have nothing to shoot that upcoming Friday. "I absolutely hated that part of this episode, and to this day I am sorry that we did it," Bea explains. "But it was the first episode of the second year, and there was nothing we could do. It was already written and scheduled."

Hunky Guest Star Alert:

Season 2, Episode #27:
Burt Reynolds in "Ladies of the Evening"
ORIGINAL AIR DATE: October 4, 1986
BLANCHE, DOROTHY, AND ROSE dress up for the premiere

BEING A FRIEND: A CONVERSATION WITH PEGGY POPE

I DID SEVERAL shows for Paul Witt and Susan Harris—a pilot, and a recurring role on *Soap*. You would never say no to them because they were so talented that their company was a gold mine. Gladys was a small but fun role, and people still come up to me and say, "I saw you last night" in a rerun—although not as much as for *9 to 5*.

In her few scenes, Gladys does seem very similar to my *9 to 5* character Margaret "Attagirl" Foster—minus the drinking problem. They're both kind of beaten down by a man in their lives. But the difference is, Gladys is a fixer, and has no problem sabotaging her pigheaded husband to appease everyone and make things work out.

They're also both kind of blunt, which is a lot like me. But it serves me well, because that's actually how I got the *9 to 5* job—I blurted something out in my audition when the writer/director Colin Higgins said I wasn't old enough for the part, and he was both taken aback and inspired to rewrite the character to fit me.

of Burt Reynolds's new movie, but are instead arrested as hookers when they stop for a drink in a hotel lobby bar. When none of them is willing to relinquish her spot at the premiere to Sophia in exchange for bail, Sophia grabs the tickets, attends the party alone—and makes fast friends with Burt Reynolds, who appears at the house at the end of the episode, ready to escort Sophia to lunch. This cameo by the top male box-office draw of the early 1980s marks the series' first big guest-star score. And if as a gay fan, you had Burt's infamous 1972 *Cosmopolitan* magazine centerfold tucked away somewhere in your sock drawer, you were especially happy to see him.

Season 2, Episode #30: "Isn't It Romantic"

WRITTEN BY: Jeffrey Duteil

DIRECTED BY: Terry Hughes

ORIGINAL AIR DATE: November 8, 1986

SYNOPSIS: Dorothy's college friend Jean (Lois Nettleton) comes to Miami to visit. It's a hard time for Jean, who recently lost her partner, Pat. As Dorothy knows, Pat was short for Patricia; Jean is a lesbian. Rose and Jean instantly find out they have a lot in common: they were both raised on dairy farms, and both love weepy movies. But problems arise when Jean finds herself surprised to admit to Dorothy that she may be falling in love with Rose. As Dorothy and Sophia worry about what to tell their naïve friend, Blanche shows herself to be not only shocked at Jean's lesbianism, but moreover jealous that Jean would prefer Rose over her. But it turns out that Dorothy may have underestimated Rose, who catches on to Jean's feelings of affection as Jean awkwardly attempts to explain them one night at bedtime. After feigning sleep to avoid the conversation, Rose tells Jean the next morning that she is flattered, and the two women decide that friendship is certainly enough.

COMMENTARY: This episode marks the first time the post-Coco *Girls* addressed the issue of homosexuality. (Well, human homosexuality, that is.) Its most famous joke in its most famous scene—where the concept of liking anything but men is so foreign to Blanche that she briefly confuses the words "lesbian" and "Lebanese"—was conceived as an in-joke referring to producer Tony Thomas's famous family.

Loaded with first-time-on-TV laughs, the episode earned 1987 Emmy nominations for Outstanding Writing in a Comedy Series and for Lois Nettleton as Outstanding Guest Performer in a Comedy Series. And after Betty White's 1986 Emmy win for Outstanding Lead Actress in a Comedy Series, Rue McClanahan took home the trophy in 1987, partly due to her performance in this episode.

MORT NATHAN: Because the show was a hit, we had the license at the time to try things that other shows couldn't do. When we would talk about gay and lesbian relationships, it wasn't so much that we wanted to do a "gay" show or an "issues" show that was controversial, but more that we thought this was an area that seemed interesting, funny, and organic to what we do. We felt there would be big laughs there, areas of unmined comedy, and we could get away with it because we were who we were. We loved taking advantage of those opportunities, like having Blanche, someone with so much sex experience, turn out to be a little ignorant of terminology and not even know the word "lesbian." It was a chance to make fun of how she thought she was sexually sophisticated. The fact that people were emotionally touched by us reaffirming gay rights or any of the social issues we brought up was an additional benefit. We weren't consciously trying to make a preachy show, but we were touched later that people appreciated what we did.

TERRY HUGHES: I didn't think of this episode as controversial when we were doing it—I just knew it was a wonderful script. The script dictated the way Jean should be played: she's just Dorothy's friend. The other ladies must not see her as anything unusual. And when we cast the role, we looked for someone who was wholesome and warm, with an accessible quality to her.

BEA ARTHUR: I love the scene in the bedroom where Blanche finds out and thinks it's outrageous that Jean prefers Rose. And it was marvelously played.

RUE MCCLANAHAN: After Blanche singing on the piano at the Rusty Anchor, that scene is my second favorite because the writing is so brilliant. Blanche has her areas of conservatism, and she obviously didn't know what a lesbian was—she didn't get the word. And then it's such a beautiful turnaround from that to being jealous. Blanche wanted to be queen again, no matter what the context. I loved that kind of thing—that's really good comedy.

BETTY WHITE: Even someone as naïve as Rose is able to sense when something is outside her ordinary realm of experience, and so she senses that Jean is attracted to her. The writers gave me that lovely speech where I talk to her in the kitchen, and I loved that they weren't afraid to cross boundaries and to go to places like that.

Season 2, Episode #36: "'Twas the Nightmare Before Christmas"

WRITTEN BY: Barry Fanaro and Mort Nathan
DIRECTED BY: Terry Hughes
ORIGINAL AIR DATE: December 20, 1986
SYNOPSIS: Rose convinces the ladies that the only way to feel the spirit of Christmas is to have an old-fashioned St. Olaf–style party before flying back to their respective hometowns. The ladies exchange gifts—with Blanche's present for each of her roommates being a calendar she has compiled of "The Men of Blanche's Boudoir." But the day after the party, when the Girls arrive to pick up Rose from work at the crisis center en route to the airport, they are held hostage by a gun-wielding psycho. Eventually Sophia comes to the rescue, with her Sicilian-bred skill of being able to tell a toy gun "from a real piece." They do arrive at the airport with only five minutes to spare before their flights, only to learn that all flights departing from Miami are cancelled due to the weather. And so, at a cheap diner, the Girls peek out at a freak Miami

BEING A FRIEND:
A CONVERSATION WITH
LOIS NETTLETON

WHEN THEY WERE casting Jean, I think what they were probably looking for was the way I actually played her, and that is, as a very straight person. Not "straight" in the sense of not being gay, but rather as an ordinary-seeming woman. I had played a gay woman one other time in the early '70s, on *Medical Center*, and had done it the same way. When Chad Everett's character told me he was in love with me, I had to tell him, I'm sorry, but I don't go that way. I think that's what they wanted for Jean, too—someone who just didn't seem stereotypically masculine in any way.

I guess this is a somewhat historic episode, but it never entered my mind to be hesitant about playing a gay woman more than any other character. After all, I would play Lady Macbeth without worrying if people would think I'm a horrible creature. I just approached Jean not by concentrating on her sexuality but by figuring out who she is as a human being. Straight or gay, we all have so many different types of relationships with other people—what are hers? Well, from that wonderful, hilarious script, you could see Jean was sensitive, outgoing, and had a good sense of humor, at ease with herself and with life. She's suffered a loss, and I've had mine, too—all I had to do was substitute a woman for a man. And it wasn't hard to imagine falling in love with Rose. It was perfectly logical, because her character was so charming and honest and innocent—the kind of person anyone can like and feel affection for.

All week during rehearsal, I laughed when I saw Rose's wonderfully funny reaction when I tell her I love her, where her eyes pop wide open facing away from me in bed. And I'll always remember the lines in the scene where Blanche confuses "lesbian" with "Lebanese," and then gets jealous that Jean picked Rose over her. The writing was great, and so were the women, getting laughs all over the place. In fact, after rehearsal one day I told my friend John Bowab that I was starting to get nervous that I wasn't getting any laughs—was I approaching this the wrong way? He told me to keep doing what I was doing, because I was there to be the "straight man." And he turned out to be right. The episode worked beautifully.

Ever since then, I've met a few gay women, and gotten some mail from others, saying how they appreciated that there wasn't anything odd about Jean, that she was gay and that was just the way she was—no big deal. Not only did quite a few of us get Emmy nominations for this episode, but it's also lovely for me to get that personal response. As an actor, to know you did something that means something to people, other than the laughs or the entertainment, means a lot.

snowstorm and realize that despite everything that went wrong, they do get to spend Christmas with their true family after all.

COMMENTARY: This episode underscores the theme of the Girls as surrogate family, which is so appealing to the Gays. But that's not why we're going to talk about it. The episode also features perhaps the most famous prop of the series other than Sophia's purse—the infamous and naughty "Men of Blanche's Boudoir" calendar—and behind-the-scenes, the series' most beloved prank. Because it turned out that thanks to the Men of *The Golden Girls* Crew, that calendar turned out even to be more of a lurid page-turner than even Blanche had counted on.

LEX PASSARIS [ASSOCIATE DIRECTOR]: In the second season, I was not yet a regular presence on the stage. But I had gotten the heads up that something fun was going to happen, and that I should come on over. It was a Thursday afternoon, when we would tape the camera run-through. And what happened next was well planned-out—the camera guys were in on it, so they even knew enough, when it came time to rehearse the scene where Blanche gives out her Christmas gifts, to turn off the time code window that blocks part of the screen. So Blanche gave wrapped boxes to the other Girls containing the calendar. But unbeknownst to them, a whole group of the production guys—stage, lighting, props, cameramen—had stayed late the night before and made up a new prop calendar, having taken some of the most provocative pictures. You could sell these in West Hollywood. They were all in just their shorts. For one shot, the prop guys got a saddle, and one lighting grip who was a huge black man bent over with the saddle on his back, and Jimmy the prop guy, who wasn't a big guy, sat on his back with a cowboy hat. And there was whipped cream.

ROBERT SPINA [SCRIPT COORDINATOR]: There were lines of dialogue as each of the ladies opened her present, so it didn't happen all at once. They were all supposed to open it and say something like, "Oh, that's lovely." Betty was the one to go first, and she kept talking as she flipped the pages, but the look on her face was, "Oh my god!" And then Bea got hers, and they all just dissolved into laughter. Bea laughed so hard that she cried for nearly five minutes. Then they each held up the calendar pages to the camera, so that we could film the pictures. It was the funniest non-aired moment in the show.

Campy Guest Star Alert:

Season 2, Episodes #37 and #44: Nancy Walker as Aunt Angela in "The Sisters" and "Long Day's Journey into Marinara"

ORIGINAL AIR DATES: January 3, 1987, and February 21, 1987

WHETHER YOU KNOW HER better as Rosie, the simple counterwoman obsessed with Bounty paper towels, or as Ida Morgenstern, *Rhoda*'s meddling mother, Nancy Walker was a TV icon. As they went nose to nose in "The Sisters" in their matching white wigs and even matching wicker purses, Sophia and Angela looked so perfectly and hilariously like long-lost sisters that the character returned only seven episodes later for a second show, "Long Day's Journey into Marinara" (where the Girls famously suspect she may have plucked and fried Rose's pet-sitting client, piano-playing chicken Count Bessie). As a result, Nancy Walker competed against two fellow *Golden Girls* guests, Lois Nettleton and Herb Edelman, for 1987's Outstanding Guest Performer in a Comedy Series Emmy; they all lost.

Appearing alongside Nancy Walker was a particular treat for Estelle Getty, although not for the reason one might initially suspect. Estelle's friend Michael Orland, now the associate musical director for *American Idol*, and her current caretaker Paul Chapdelaine both remember her eagerly looking forward to taping the first Aunt Angela episode. "Estelle told me how for years when she lived in New York, she was Nancy Walker's stand-in for those Bounty commercials," Michael remembers. "And Nancy never gave her the time of day. She wasn't mean, but she never went out of her way to talk to Estelle. So when Nancy got booked on *The Golden Girls*, Estelle was excited, and started plotting how she was going to go up and say something to her. But then the moment Nancy walked onto the set, and now it was Nancy coming onto Estelle's show, Estelle said she no longer felt the need to bring it up. So she never did."

Hunky Guest Star Alert:

Season 2, Episode #46: Mario Lopez in "Dorothy's Prize Pupil"

ORIGINAL AIR DATE: March 14, 1987

THIS EPISODE GUEST STARS a very young Mario Lopez as the promising student whom Dorothy helps to win a writing contest, inadvertently signaling the INS that he's an illegal alien from Cuba. Lopez, of course, went on to star in the 1997 Greg Louganis biopic *Breaking the Surface*, where he showed washboard abs and a friendliness to the gay community, and currently appears as Dr. Christian Ramirez on the CBS soap *The Bold and the Beautiful*. But take a look here and see if you can detect, two years before he became "Slater" on *Saved by the Bell*, Mario's future hotness. So what if he was only thirteen years old at the time of this episode. As Dorothy would say, "Who are you to judge?"

Hunky Guest Star Alert:

Season 2, Episode #49: George Clooney in "To Catch a Neighbor"

ORIGINAL AIR DATE: May 2, 1987

BEFORE HE WAS *ER*'s Dr. Douglas Ross or Booker on *Roseanne*, and just as he finished a career-building stint as handyman George on *The Facts of Life*,

George Clooney was police officer Bobby Hopkins, who joined a stakeout at 5161 Richmond Street and spent a sleepover being doted on by four grandmother figures who looked like they'd be more than happy to tuck him in at night.

Season 3, Episode #58: "Strange Bedfellows"

WRITTEN BY: Christopher Lloyd

DIRECTED BY: Terry Hughes

ORIGINAL AIR DATE: November 7, 1987

SYNOPSIS: As the ladies wrap up a campaign party for Gil Kessler, candidate for city councilman, they find a forgotten folder. Blanche is elected to take the folder over to his house, only to be "caught" by the press, who turn the photo into a major scandal, since Kessler is a married man. Blanche insists that nothing happened, but becomes deeply hurt when, knowing her appetite for men, her roommates don't believe her. Only when Kessler himself eventually refutes the story do the other Girls realize they owe Blanche an apology. And apparently now hooked on honesty, Kessler decides that he should also admit to the sex-change operation in his past: he used to be a she—but neither of them now has a shot at winning the city council chair.

COMMENTARY: Interestingly, although this episode touches on transsexualism, it does so only as an ending beat for a story that is actually about the hurt feelings that come from friendship betrayed.

Its writer, Christopher Lloyd (*not* the *Taxi* and *Back to the Future* actor), began his writing career as an apprentice on *The Golden Girls*, then moved up the writers' ranks, eventually becoming an executive producer on the gay-sensibility-infused hit *Frasier*.

CHRISTOPHER LLOYD: For this episode, we originally had a different ending, but then we sort of pasted this together. At some points in the story Gil had to allude to a "secret" so that the Girls could take that to mean an affair he was having with Blanche. And originally, he had some other dark secret, although I don't remember what it was. The episode had a good issue at its center, an emotional place where Blanche's roommates didn't believe her because of her reputation. But the ending is often where all the hard work comes in storytelling, and I think if there was a fault in the writing of *The Golden Girls*, it was that sometimes there could be a sort of slap-dash ending to some of the episodes. This one even at the time seemed slightly unsatisfying.

RUE MCCLANAHAN: The reason Blanche gets so upset in this episode is because her dearest friends are calling her a liar. There's no way she can prove that she's telling the truth, and it's very painful and devastating. This one was easy to do because those emotions were very clear and true the way they were written. It was also easy to have a crush on John Schuck, who played Gil Kessler. I thought that it was a delicious piece of casting, that he was once a woman, and John played that with such subtlety and humor. It may not be politically correct how the ending suggests that because he's a transsexual he can't get elected, but that is still going on today.

Season 3, Episode #64: "The Artist"

WRITTEN BY: Christopher Lloyd
DIRECTED BY: Terry Hughes
ORIGINAL AIR DATE: December 19, 1987
SYNOPSIS: When Blanche's museum client Laszlo drops her off at home, she has some exciting news: the artist has asked her to pose nude for one of his sculptures. But when Blanche catches sight of some sketches for the piece and declares that they look like a "hideous, wrinkled, old bag," the truth comes out that Laszlo has made the same request of Rose and Dorothy as well. After all three smitten ladies continue to pose for the artist, the day of the big unveiling arrives. Although the statue does not look identifiably like any of them, Laszlo explains that he has imbued his creation with Rose's sweetness, Blanche's sensuality, and Dorothy's strength. "It is all of you," he tells them. "It's not hard to understand why you are such good friends. You complement each other very well." As the ladies are left to marvel at the amalgam, gallery owner Victor sashays by. "It looks like we're a hit," he tells Laszlo, winking. The Girls' faces show their realization that the artist for whom they've agreed to pose only out of lust is in fact gay. "I'm sorry, I thought you knew," says Laszlo.
COMMENTARY: This third-season episode is structured strikingly like the Season Two episode "The Actor," in which the Girls all competed for the attention of

their director as they appeared in a local production of an *Our Town*-esque play. But here, there's a new twist ending: the object of their affection turns out to be gay. Like the Girls, we learn this only at the end, after a brief and mincing declaration from a man who is obviously Laszlo's lover. It's a challenging assignment for the actor playing Victor, the lover: to convey within just five not-particularly-gay words such an obvious degree of homosexuality that the entire audience is guaranteed to get the joke.

CHRISTOPHER LLOYD: More than in the "Strange Bedfellows" episode, I think the ending of this one makes sense and is integrated well into the story. In retrospect, you are saying that Laszlo is gay and therefore he wasn't really leading these women on this whole time. It was really just their egos and the idea of being a muse for a great artist that was carrying them away. So I don't think the revelation that Laszlo is gay feels like a *deus ex machina* kind of moment. The character who delivers the revealing line wasn't a key character—he was only there to deliver information, and it had to be delivered quickly. Perhaps we could have asked him to play it a little less strongly and the audience would have still picked up on it.

TERRY HUGHES: I just saw this episode again recently, and I was sort of uncomfortable how the gay character played at the end. I think we may have overdone it, and I take responsibility for that one.

Campy Guest Star Alert:

Season 3, Episode #75: Alice Ghostley as Mrs. Zbornak in "Mother's Day"

ORIGINAL AIR DATE: May 7, 1988

PERHAPS BEST-KNOWN as *Designing Women*'s memory-challenged matron Bernice Clifton or as *Bewitched*'s bumbling Esmeralda, Alice Ghostley is, if not a gay icon, at least gay-icon-adjacent as a frequent on-screen foil for, and off-screen friend of, Paul Lynde. Here she plays Mrs. Zbornak, Dorothy's tough-as-nails mother-in-law who secretly shares her daughter-in-law's frustration with Stan, that perennial yutz. But don't get too excited—Alice's role constitutes an all-too-brief appearance in this "wraparound" show featuring each Girl in a separate Mother's Day-themed vignette.

Season 4, Episode #82: "Sophia's Wedding, Part 1"

WRITTEN BY: Barry Fanaro & Mort Nathan

DIRECTED BY: Terry Hughes

ORIGINAL AIR DATE: November 19, 1988

SYNOPSIS: When Sophia's old friend Esther Weinstock passes away, Sophia at first refuses to attend the funeral in Brooklyn out of resentment for Esther's husband Max (Jack Gilford). According to Sophia, forty years ago Max ruined the pizza-and-knish business he and Sophia's late husband Salvadore had founded in Coney Island by gambling away a week's receipts. But after Dorothy nudges Sophia into going to the funeral, the truth comes out: it was Sal who was the gambler, and Max who bravely covered for him all these years to save Sophia's marriage. Sophia immediately sees Max in a new light—and back home in Miami, she even gets caught in bed with him. Now in love, the two decide to marry.

Meanwhile, Rose's application to start an unauthorized chapter of the Elvis Presley Hunka-Hunka-Burnin'-Love Fan Club has been approved. But as membership begins to sag, Blanche realizes that what the club really needs is an Elvis impersonator.

Unable to accept that her mother is about to marry a man she has hated for so long, Dorothy at first refuses to give her blessing to the union. On the day of the wedding, Sophia locks herself in the bathroom, wondering if Dorothy may be right. Max—and the extremely gay caterer (Raye Birk)— both try to coax her into going through with the wedding, to no avail. It is only Dorothy's realization that she is selfishly guarding the memory of her late father and her subsequent blessing that convinces Sophia to proceed with the wedding. But there's just one problem: Rose has confused her mailing lists, and now all of Sophia and Max's wedding guests are Elvis impersonators.

COMMENTARY: This episode introduces Raye Birk's gay caterer character, who proved popular enough to be brought back two seasons later when Dorothy nearly remarries Stan in "There Goes the Bride."

It is also remembered for the scene where Dorothy comes across the disturbing visual of her mother and Max post-coitally in bed together, enjoying, as Sophia puts it, "Afterglow."

And notably only in retrospect, "Sophia's Wedding, Part 1" features an early and rare acting appearance by one of today's hippest writer/directors. No, you're not seeing things; yes, that *is* Quentin Tarantino as an Elvis impersonator. Back row, center.

MORT NATHAN: In the '80s, wedding episodes were very popular. The network always wanted weddings, and we loved the simultaneous absurdity and reality of an 82-year-old woman in a white wedding gown. We liked getting to that emotional area of a daughter having to give a blessing to her mother, of a man replacing her father. We thought it was a fun area to explore. As far as Quentin Tarantino goes, I read an article about him when he first became a phenomenon as the director of *Pulp Fiction*. He was talking about how he got started in the business and broke in as an actor, and he said that one of the early things he did was *The Golden Girls*. So I went back and took out some stills of this episode, and there he was. I had no idea he had been one of the Elvises.

RUE MCCLANAHAN: Raye Birk practically had me on the floor laughing, he was so funny. And I love the line that Blanche says to him so much. It's terribly funny, and deliciously right for her to say in the moment. And I don't think she says it in a nasty or homophobic way. She just says it in a funny way.

BEING A FRIEND:
A CONVERSATION WITH
RAYE BIRK

WHEN I FIRST heard about the role of the caterer from my agents, they passed along the breakdown they had received which said something like "42-year-old caterer, gay, in four scenes." So right from the beginning I knew the character was supposed to be gay, and I didn't have any problem with that—I'd played lots of gay characters in the theater. I got the "sides," and I liked the character and thought he was funny, because he had another dimension to him. I thought he was sweet and sentimental, and that made me feel better that this character's hallmark isn't just that he's gay. They were trying to do something with the character.

Certainly there were laugh lines about the fact that he's gay. In one scene, Blanche turns to me and has a line, "You're ready to fly right outta here, aren't you?" It had been in the script from the beginning, and was very successful all throughout the process. The writers loved it, and it ended up paying off big with the audience—a huge laugh.

But the show went through a lot of changes and rewrites in the course of five days, and we lost some of the elements of the character that I really liked. He originally had a lot of lines where he talked about 1940s movie stars, and I thought those had been terrific because they showed a sweet and emotional side to the character. I was upset, and went to the producers and writers and said I don't think I want to do this role, because you're reducing it to something that's just a stereotype. I have gay friends, and I'd feel bad doing this clichéd version of a character. No judgment about you guys, but maybe you need to have another actor to do this. And to their credit, they had a conference and restored most of the dialogue. Of course as I recall, in the edit room they cut stuff anyway, probably for time. But what was interesting to me was that they were sympathetic to my point of view about the character, and I really appreciated that.

In the end, my gay friends liked the performance, which I took as a high compliment. And I don't get recognized often, but a few times when I've worked in San Francisco, gay audience members have come up and said, "I loved you on *The Golden Girls*. I thought your caterer was just wonderful." Obviously they didn't have a problem with how he came across, which is a compliment for both me and the writers.

Season 4, Episode #85: "Scared Straight"

WRITTEN BY: Christopher Lloyd

DIRECTED BY: Terry Hughes

ORIGINAL AIR DATE: December 10, 1988

SYNOPSIS: When Blanche's baby brother Clayton Hollingsworth (Monte Markham) arrives for a visit, the Girls find themselves face-to-face with a male version of the Southern belle: charming, good-looking, and on the prowl—for men. Yes, Clayton is gay—a fact he confesses to Rose after running into her in the park after he ditches the woman with whom his sister had set him up on an uncomfortable blind date. Rose encourages Clayton to come out to his sister, and he initially agrees. But when he comes home to a querulous Blanche, he instead blurts out that he and Rose slept together. Blanche hates the thought of her brother dating Rose, and harasses Rose until Clayton finally is forced to reveal the truth. Blanche initially refuses to believe it, but eventually comes around to accepting that she and her brother may just have the same excellent taste in men.

COMMENTARY: There was briefly a gay houseboy, there was a lesbian college friend, and a gay caterer. But this episode marks the first time someone in one of the Girls' families has turned out to be Family. Storywise, the episode is very similar to a landmark 1972 episode of the *Mary Tyler Moore Show*. In "My Brother's

Keeper," directed by Jay Sandrich, the gay brother nosy landlady Phyllis Lindstrom (Cloris Leachman pretends to date Rhoda (Valerie Harper) rather than be forced to come out to his sister. That episode ends differently: in a clever twist, Phyllis is not devastated to hear that her brother is gay, because that is at least preferable to him dating "that awful Rhoda."

It makes sense that the two shows would do similar episodes because after all, playing gay and coming-out for laughs is a time-honored tradition. "Scared Straight" writer Christopher Lloyd, whose father David wrote for *Mary Tyler Moore*, remembers hearing how the late Robert Moore, the actor (and later five-time Tony-nominated director) playing Phyllis's brother Ben Sutherland, became worried the night of the episode's filming that the audience was not going to laugh at his gay character. "And his lover said something to him along the lines of, 'Honey, you've got nothing to worry about. They've been laughing at fags since Aristophanes—you're gonna kill 'em.' He went out there and of course the audience ate it up."

CHRISTOPHER LLOYD: We frequently rolled in relatives to upset the stasis of the household and be a jumping-off point for stories. A gay relative seemed like a natural idea for the show, and perfect for Blanche. Dorothy is from Brooklyn, so it would have shocked her less, but Blanche is not only the most sexual of the characters, but you could say she is the most fiercely heterosexual. Plus, she's from the South and rather traditional. So it would rock her the most to have a gay person within

And of course, we could play on the idea ~~and~~ her brother both liking guys, which ~~w~~uld be a fun avenue to go down. We ~~h~~ave our cake and eat it too in this show—we could do our gay jokes, and then have a nice, tidy, lovely ending where Blanche embraces her brother and everyone is happy. I think that this episode has resonance because of the Girls' characters. These are women who grew up in an era when they were a little bit discriminated against, when women were second-class citizens. And now they are being re-discriminated against because they're women in their sixties, who are a little bit outcast in society. So they can speak a message of tolerance, from a place where they know what they are talking about.

RUE MCCLANAHAN: I semi-enjoyed doing this episode. What I mean is, it wasn't my favorite, because it was very hard to play. I'm not homophobic and Blanche was, somewhat—certainly when it came to her brother. I'm just glad she came around.

BETTY WHITE: One of Rose's better qualities was her total lack of duplicity. It comes into play here as it did in so many of the shows. She's never sarcastic, and never any of those "smarter" things. It was her total honesty and innocence that made her a safe confidante for Clayton.

Season 4, Episode #92: "Valentine's Day"
WRITTEN BY: Kathy Speer, Terry Grossman, Barry Fanaro, and Mort Nathan
DIRECTED BY: Terry Hughes

ORIGINAL AIR DATE: February 11, 1989

SYNOPSIS: When Dorothy's, Rose's, and then Blanche's dates cancel on Valentine's Day, they join Sophia—whom they don't believe when she claims to have a date with Julio Iglesias—around the table, eating chocolates and reminiscing about Valentines past. Sophia claims to have witnessed the St. Valentine's Day Massacre while stopped in a Chicago auto garage with her father and husband, Sal, on a cross-country trip. Rose takes the heat for the time she mistakenly booked the three Girls at a mountaintop nudist resort. Blanche reminisces about the time she inadvertently coached a gay man on how to propose to his boyfriend. And Dorothy blushes even remembering the time the Girls made a spectacle of themselves buying condoms to bring on a cruise. Finally, the doorbell rings: it's dates Edgar, Raymond, and Steve, who with Sophia's help were just pulling a romantic Valentine's Day surprise. Dinner and dancing await all but Sophia, who runs to the back door to let in Julio, from whom she gets a serenade of "Begin the Beguine."

COMMENTARY: In *Golden Girls* parlance, a "wraparound" show is made up of four independent vignettes, tied together by a frame story which usually involves someone saying "Remember the time when–?" They are a standard writer's trick; the vignettes can be divided among the staff and cranked out more quickly than a more involved single storyline. But for viewers, they normally stink.

But not this one. "Valentine's Day," written by the show's four executive producers at the time, is a comedy treasure trove—not to mention a gay gold mine as well. It contains not one but two of the most beloved moments in the entire series. In the first, the Girls accidentally book a package at a clothing-optional resort. But just when they steel up their nerve to join the natives *au naturale*, they arrive in the dining room, only to notice that they're the only ones who are naked. "Ladies," a waiter says derisively. "We always dress for dinner."

In the second famous moment, *The Golden Girls* became one of the first sitcoms to promote safe sex, with an infamous and hilarious vignette where the Girls somewhat embarrassedly purchase condoms. True to form, it is Blanche who reminds the Girls as they pick up sundries for an upcoming romantic cruise to the Bahamas that, to be safe and socially responsible, they ought to buy some "protection." Dorothy and Rose are initially embarrassed to buy condoms, but ultimately agree that Blanche is right.

MORT NATHAN: We flat-out stole the idea for the condom scene from Woody Allen's *Take the Money and Run*, a movie that I saw as a kid and thought it was hilarious. I remember the joke I loved—Woody Allen asking for a "price check on an orgasm." Ours had different situations and joke constructions, but it was an homage to that specifically. The reason we went down that road is because we thought we could really top it, like with the line about Rose accidentally picking up the extra-sensitive condoms in black. I don't know if it's because we were a hit that we got away with doing that kind of material, or if the censors missed it, or if we negotiated with them for it. But they let us get away with some stuff.

• • •

IN YET A third fun vignette, Blanche makes her annual visit to the bar where George proposed to her over champagne, still following the tradition even now that he's gone. As she explains her request for two glasses to the waiter, a man at the bar overhears and remarks on the romance of it all. When he mentions that he is at the bar because he himself is about to propose, Blanche realizes that they two were meant to meet, so that she could coach him to propose the same beautiful way George popped the question to her.

But little does Blanche know, the object of her pupil's affections is a man. That revelation may have been meant merely as a punchline, but this small moment, sandwiched among other stories in the episode, presaged the current gay marriage issue by more than seventeen years.

But wait, there's more. As if all that weren't enough, this episode sets off another Hunky Guest Star Alert. From the very beginning we've known that the Girls are heavy into Julio Iglesias—in the show's pilot, Dorothy uses tickets to his concert in an attempt to lure a depressed Blanche out of her bedroom when her intended husband turns out to be a bigamist. Now, three and a half years later, it's Sophia who lands him, as a Valentine's Day date no less. Having lunched with Burt Reynolds and now dining with Julio at Wolfie's, that old lady definitely gets the hottest dates.

BEING A FRIEND: A CONVERSATION WITH MONTE MARKHAM

WHEN I GOT the script for "Scared Straight," I thought it was well written and funny as hell. I'd known Betty White and Paul Witt since the late '60s, so doing the show would be like old home week. And I never thought twice about playing gay or being typecast—if I were to do that, then I'm in the wrong business. It was always about the work. And with work I always say, never put anything on film that you don't want to see forever. With *The Golden Girls*, you knew those writers and producers and that cast and that director were going to do it right.

We went through several rewrites, and I actually thought the first draft had had funnier lines. Sometimes they fix these things to death. In the first draft, when Rose finally figures out that Clayton is gay, she had a line, "Are you... light in the loafers?" She was obviously quoting things she'd heard that she took too literally and didn't really understand.

I remember that during a break after the first act, someone in the audience asked the warm-up comic, "Is Monte Markham gay?" The warm-up answered no, and the same guy said, "But he's playing a gay character!" And I remember the warm-up guy answering back, "If he were playing a murderer, would you think he is one?"

They brought me back to do another one, "Sisters of the Bride," where Clayton was getting married to his boyfriend. I remember near the end, there's a scene where I tell Blanche that I would do anything for my boyfriend, "and he would bend over backwards for me." Bea was sitting on the couch, and just put her hand over Estelle's mouth. And the audience started laughing, and kept laughing until finally we had to stop tape. Just the idea of what Estelle would have said was the funniest joke the writers could have written.

Since then, a lot of people have come up to me and said "I saw you on *The Golden Girls*," and it has become a running joke with me— that turns out to be as much as saying "and I'm gay." Paul Witt told me that they dropped that first episode into several syndication cycles because it's one of the most popular, so it plays very often.

I've answered every piece of fan mail I've ever gotten about *The Golden Girls*. People really respond to the dignity of Clayton's character, and I'd like to say the role was groundbreaking— the word actually reminds me of the only time I ever went to a political fundraiser, and Billy Crystal was on the dais, back when he was on *Soap*. Someone introduced him as playing a "groundbreaking gay character." (I remember he looked over at me and gave his funny smile, shrugged modestly, and said, "It's a living.") I'd like to think of Clayton as historic like that.

At the time, I looked at him mostly as a funny acting role. That's the nature of coming from the theater—you take the good, funny roles, which are so damn few and far between. But I also realize it was as much a terrific role as it was socially important at the time.

NINA WASS (PRODUCER): Julio Iglesias was supposed to come in at the tag and serenade Sophia. But when he arrived, he said he didn't want to sing. I assumed he didn't feel like he was in good voice. I was concerned that Paul and Tony would be upset, but Estelle bailed me out. She said, "Honey, I'll take care of it." Estelle had always had her own issues with stage fright, and so she was so compassionate for someone feeling apprehensive that she was able to take care of him in that moment. And so she took his arm, and she sang to him—and that's the way you see it in the episode.

Campy Guest Star Alert:

Season 4, Episode #93: The Del Rubio Triplets in "You Gotta Have Hope"

ORIGINAL AIR DATE: February 25, 1989

THINGS DON'T GO WELL when Dorothy takes charge of planning a hospital charity show. First of all, she thinks that all the available acts stink. Well, Dorothy may not be a fan of the kitschy Del Rubio triplets and their version of the Pointer Sisters' "Neutron Dance," but we Gays sure are. The three identical guitar-strumming ladies—Elena, Eadie, and Milly Del Rubio—popped up on various shows of the late '80s and early '90s, most notably *Pee-Wee's Playhouse*, each time putting their own strange, unique spin on the pop tunes of the day. This episode's co-writer, Mort Nathan, explains that he and partner Barry Fanaro had seen the ladies perform, and wrote them into *The Golden Girls* because after all, here are three old ladies with a hip, cult following. "In addition to mainstream stunt casting," Mort explains, "we would also try to go with some more esoteric choices."

Oh yeah, this episode also featured some guy named Bob Hope as the charity show emcee (whom Rose always fantasized, as she was growing up in the orphanage, was her father). You may have heard of him. Apparently he's famous for things he did throughout his life in front of a whole bunch of servicemen.

Campy Guest Star Alert:

Season 4, Episode #95: Anne Francis in "Til Death Do We Volley"

ORIGINAL AIR DATE: March 18, 1989

THIS EPISODE FEATURES Anne Francis—a favorite of lesbians since her days as the sexy, self-sufficient title character in the 1965–66 ABC detective series *Honey West*—as Dorothy's prankster high-school friend, Trudy McMann. Here, Anne trades in her pet ocelot for a tennis racket, and in a move worthy of private-eye Honey, fakes her own death-by-heart-attack on the tennis court.

Season 5, Episode #121: "An Illegitimate Concern"

WRITTEN BY: Marc Cherry & Jamie Wooten
DIRECTED BY: Terry Hughes
ORIGINAL AIR DATE: February 12, 1990
SYNOPSIS: When a mysterious young man claiming to be an encyclopedia salesman shows up looking for Blanche's late husband George, the ladies become suspicious when he doesn't actually try to sell them any encyclopedias. A few days later, they spot him at the supermarket, and Dorothy spies him waiting outside the house in his car. Although Rose assumes he's a "sex-crazed psycho with a Granny complex," Blanche decides to confront him and his obvious obsession with her. When she does, she gets quite a shock: the young man, David, claims to be George's illegitimate son. Outraged, Blanche kicks him out of the house.

Meanwhile, Sophia persuades Dorothy to enter the Shady Pines mother/daughter beauty pageant so she can finally beat her archenemy Gladys Goldfine. They roll in a piano and practice their talent: a duet of "I Got You, Babe" dressed as Sonny and Cher.

Trying to comfort Blanche, Dorothy and Sophia tell her about their own husbands' infidelities, and all conclude that "men are scum." Even Rose later admits that Charlie cheated on her, too, and advises Blanche not to throw away all the good memories due to one mistake. When David returns one last time begging Blanche for information about his father, she concedes, and the two of them go through her old photo album, from which she gives him a picture of George on a fishing trip. She realizes she was taking her anger at George out on David, who is actually a very nice man.

Sophia and Dorothy return home from the beauty pageant as runners-up, but feeling victorious—they beat Gladys Goldfine, who sang "Try to Remember"— but couldn't.

COMMENTARY: This episode contains one of the series' most famous gags, a visual so perfect it will stay with you forever. Bea Arthur and Estelle Getty, as Dorothy and Sophia, impersonating Sonny and Cher brilliantly. Much of the credit for making this storyline work must go to the show's costume designer, Judy Evans Steele, whose work in transforming the two actresses into the famous 1970s husband-and-wife singing duo Bea calls "incredible." In its larger, "A" plot, the episode also features actor Mark Moses, the future *Desperate Housewives* creepy hubby Paul Young, as George's somewhat creepy illegitimate son David.

JAMIE WOOTEN: When Marc and I were thinking up ideas to pitch to *The Golden Girls*, we knew they hadn't done a lot with dead husbands. And by the time a show has gotten to season five, you know they've obviously thought of all the normal stories, so we decided to go way out. We wanted to think of a story where something that happened to George could affect Blanche's life today. Once we had that, the story became kind of obvious to us, and we couldn't believe they hadn't come up with it yet. We pitched ten stories, and once they heard this one, they said, "That's it." But the interesting thing is, although we pitched it with a mother/daughter pageant as the B story, the Sonny and Cher part was not in it. Marc and I later came up with that on our own, and we didn't ask them if we could do it—we just put it in. We ran the risk that they could have gotten it and said, "What the hell is this Sonny and Cher thing?" But I think taking that risk is actually what got us on staff.

MARC CHERRY: I've always been fascinated by people's pasts coming back to haunt them. So the idea that Blanche finding out that her dead husband had had an affair was, I thought, an interesting story idea. Just recently, Lifetime did their big retrospective of the show and asked each of the ladies to name their favorite episode and favorite musical moment. I was so honored because Rue's favorite musical moment was the episode Jamie and I wrote, "Journey to the Center of Attention," where Blanche sings atop the piano, and Bea's was doing "I Got You, Babe" with Estelle.

BEA ARTHUR: I had never done a Cher impersonation before, but of course I had seen her, so I picked up the hair flip and the tongue thing that I did in this episode. I actually was very upset that we didn't get to do more than we did with it, because I loved it. I loved seeing Estelle with that little furry jacket and the moustache on.

TERRY HUGHES: Once Bea entered in the Cher costume, the audience reaction was so loud that she had to stand there and vamp, just picking at her hair while waiting for the laugh to die down. She had a whole scene to do, but she had to wait before she could go any further into it.

Season 5, Episode #122: "72 Hours"

WRITTEN BY: Richard Vaczy & Tracy Gamble
DIRECTED BY: Terry Hughes
ORIGINAL AIR DATE: February 17, 1990
SYNOPSIS: Rose receives a letter from the hospital where she had her gallbladder removed, warning that during her transfusion she might have been exposed to blood containing HIV antibodies. As the ladies accompany her to the hospital for an AIDS test, Blanche comforts a very frightened Rose by explaining that she too has had the test and knows what Rose is going through. But after checking out fine physically, Rose is surprised to learn that she must wait three days for the test results.

Unable to sleep, Rose begins to become hysterical, leading the ladies to realize how traumatic waiting for the test results can be. They discuss times when they've had to wait and were afraid, then vow to help Rose through whatever comes along—even though, as Sophia points out, it's scary when the disease is so close to home. The seventy-two hours finally over, the girls all breathe a sigh of relief as Rose finds out that she's fine.

BEHIND THE SCENES: A CONVERSATION WITH TRACY GAMBLE

THIS EPISODE was based on a true story that had happened to my mother. She got notified that if you had had a transfusion in this certain period of time, you had to get checked. She and my dad were scared to death. It ended up fine, and she knew that the odds were against there being anything wrong. But it was hell to sweat out those seventy-two hours until she got the results.

My writing partner Richard Vaczy and I thought it would be a good storyline for Rose, partly because the audience might view her—and she views herself—as the last person who might have to worry about HIV. After all, she's just a goody-two-shoes from Minnesota. We also liked how with the four characters, everyone could have a different opinion about the subject, which would be a good way to raise issues we wanted to raise while still being entertaining. So, Rose had the common reaction of thinking, "I've never been bad—why did this happen to me?" And when she lashes out and says to Blanche, "You must have gone to bed with hundreds of men. All I had was one innocent operation!" and Blanche's reaction is, "Hey, wait a minute—are you saying this should be me and not you?" it raises questions of what is "good" and what is "bad" and what does it matter, anyway? As Blanche reminds her, "AIDS is not a bad person's disease, Rose. It is not God punishing people for their sins." She's saying that just because I'm promiscuous, that doesn't mean I'm a "bad" person.

Before we started writing, Richard and I talked to HIV experts at UCLA and asked what was the information they'd like us to put across. At that time, there was a cottage industry of testing centers where people could walk in, and then would call up days later for the results. And while it was good that people were getting tested, the UCLA people stressed that there needs to be counseling for people when they get their results, whether they're positive or negative. So we were happy that this episode became an opportunity to get the message out there that, positive or negative, you need a support group—which is what we have the doctor say to Rose when he says that she's fine. In Rose's case, she has the built-in support group of Dorothy, Blanche, and Sophia. They were the ones to help her make it through the three-day waiting period and all of the denial and panic. And they did it by letting her know that no matter what the test results might be, Rose was going to be okay because she was loved.

As happy as we were to be doing the episode, I do remember that that week, people both at the show and at the network didn't like it— everyone was very nervous. But once it was shot and aired, we started getting a lot of acclaim. We got a lot of supportive letters, even from within the industry, from people whose sister, brother, or other family member had died of HIV. We got a commendation from the Centers for Disease Control, and we even were contacted by the organization Women in Film letting us know that if we were to submit ourselves for their award, we would win. They thought from my first name that I was a woman, and when they found out I wasn't, they said to submit it with a female producer's name on the script. But Richard and I went through too much shit to get it on the air, and weren't about to put anybody else's name on it—we were too proud. It ended up being a very good show to have done.

COMMENTARY: Again capitalizing on its license to tackle hot social issues, *The Golden Girls* was among the first sitcoms to suggest that HIV and AIDS was a problem for everyone, not just the gay community.

RICHARD VACZY: Tracy and I really loved the idea of showing what must that time be like between knowing something might be wrong and finding out what it is. And with the theater backgrounds of everyone on the show and the people they knew with HIV and AIDS, we thought everyone would appreciate and therefore love it. We guessed wrong. It turned out to be the darkest week I ever experienced on that stage, because the material hit so close to home with people. And we ended up doing a lot of work on the script, mostly because we came to realize that inherently, if you're waiting out a seventy-two-hour period, there's no story going on other than waiting. We started to realize that as we were writing it, but we wanted to do the show anyway because we thought it was important.

BETTY WHITE: Not only were people understandably afraid of AIDS, but a lot of people wouldn't even admit it existed. So this was a daring episode to do, and the writers went straight for it. It's interesting that they picked Rose for that situation—Blanche was such a busy lady, but if it had been her story it would have taken on a whole other color. But with Rose being Miss Not-Always-With-It, it came as a real surprise. And I know it sounds corny to say, but I'm proud that there was a little learning in this episode. I think the audience went away knowing a little more about the subject than they knew going in.

Campy Guest Star Alert:

Season 6, Episode #136: Kathleen Freeman as Mother Superior, and Lynne Stewart as Sister Anne in "How Do You Solve a Problem Like Sophia?"

ORIGINAL AIR DATE: November 10, 1990

KATHLEEN FREEMAN, who played Mother Superior in this episode, was a veteran TV, film, and stage character actress who found one of her biggest successes just before her death in 2001, receiving a Tony nomination

BEING A FRIEND: A CONVERSATION WITH LYNNE STEWART

I HAD ALWAYS heard that the guest players on *The Golden Girls* didn't get any of the funny lines, but that wasn't my experience. I had a small part and had one big laugh, and everyone was very supportive. I was a fan of the show—and actually I still watch on Lifetime—and it was amazing working with Kathleen Freeman and with Betty White, whose show I had watched as a young girl and who had such a joy to her in performing that I remember saying that I wanted to do that, to be her. And I adore Bea Arthur, and desperately wanted to establish contact with her. Paul Reubens had worked with her, and so he suggested I give her his love. I went up and said I had been on *Pee-Wee's Playhouse,* and from that point on, she always said, "Hello, dear" to me whenever she passed, and was so sweet.

It was also so much fun playing a nun—and actually, every once in a while in an interview someone will recognize me from this episode, despite the habit. And that habit was much more comfortable than being dressed up in Miss Yvonne drag, with the high heels and corset and huge wig which made me unrecognizable in a different way.

for her role in the Broadway version of *The Full Monty*. And if her subordinate Sister Anne looks familiar to you but you can't quite place her, try picturing her minus the habit and plus a hairdo that's even taller. Yes, that's none other than Lynne Stewart—Miss Yvonne from *Pee-Wee's Playhouse*!

MARC CHERRY: With Kathleen Freeman, I felt like I was working with a piece of TV history. But there were so many of those on *The Golden Girls*, you got kind of jaded. One of my favorite things about doing this episode was researching it, because we met with a woman who had been married and had a family, and then became a nun at age fifty-five. She said one of the things the Church did was psychological testing, so that Rorschach ink-blot test in the episode is actually based on truth.

The show actually got sued by the Church of Scientology for this episode. There had been a joke where the Mother Superior asks Sophia why she found a copy of *Dianetics* in her room. And Sophia says, "*Dianetics*? I thought it said 'Diuretics!'" The Scientologists sued, and Paul and Tony realized it was cheaper to settle than to fight it in court.

Campy Guest Star Alert:

Season 6, Episode #137:
Sonny Bono and Lyle Waggoner in "Mrs. George Devereaux"
ORIGINAL AIR DATE: November 17, 1990

IN "MRS. GEORGE DEVEREAUX," things get weird at 5161 Richmond: first it turns out that Blanche's late husband may be alive after all, and then stranger yet, Dorothy has her choice of two different men! Oh wait, that's not the strange part, this is: the men are Sonny Bono and 1970s TV heartthrob Lyle Waggoner (!), whose campy cameos offset a very touching A story for Blanche. Eventually, Dorothy picks Sonny—and Blanche wakes up, revealing that the whole episode has been a dream. And a recurring dream at that, one which has haunted her quite often lately. But this time, she tells Dorothy, it was a good dream, because it ended differently: she got to hug George one last time.

RUE MCCLANAHAN: I love this episode, because it has a lot of heart, and a really satisfying resolution. I love having George come back into the script from time to time, because I love what it says about Blanche: she's truly still in love with him. It's a very satisfying, meaty thing to play as an actor.

Season 6, Episode #138: Cesar Romero in "Girls Just Wanna Have Fun... Before They Die"

WRITTEN BY: Gail Parent & Jim Vallely
DIRECTED BY: Matthew Diamond
ORIGINAL AIR DATE: November 24, 1990
SYNOPSIS: Sophia has the hots for Tony DelVecchio (Cesar Romero), so she enlists Blanche's help in making her irresistible for their upcoming date.

The date does go well—so well, in fact, that in a postcoital moment in bed, Sophia gets caught up in the moment and lets slip the "L word." Unfortunately, Tony's response is a little lacking; all he can manage is "I care for you." Furious, Sophia storms home, only to be chastised by Blanche for divulging her feelings too quickly. As Sophia laments that all she wanted was for a man to say "I love you" one more time, Blanche offers further advice. But Sophia decides to stop playing games and instead confronts Tony, who confesses that he hasn't expressed affection for a woman since his wife died. He finally does say, "I do love you," and they kiss, settling in for a pleasant evening of looking at old family photos.

COMMENTARY: This episode offers a rare glimpse into Sophia's sex life, showing her in bed with a man without that visual itself being the joke. Of course that man was Cesar Romero (Campy Guest Star Alert!), otherwise known for his lavender suit and his propensity to wear waaay too much makeup. But stripped of all the Joker's accoutrements, it turns out that Cesar Romero's Tony is rather endearingly shy and romantic.

MARC CHERRY: Jim Vallely's original joke was, "I took an eighty-five year old woman, and made her look like a sixty-five-year-old gay man," but the censor wouldn't let us say it. He thought that we were saying that all gay men are drag queens or wear dresses. Immediately, our showrunner Marc Sotkin turned to Jamie and me and said, "You're gay—get on the phone with this guy." It was a fascinating moment for me, because I never thought of Jamie or myself as "the gay writers," but in that moment they suddenly needed a spokesman, and looked to us right away. It stunned me to realize that when they look at me they first see "gay guy," but I didn't mind. So I got on the phone and said to the censor, "I'm gay, but I am not offended by this joke." And the censor, who was not gay, was so protective that despite my arguing and arguing, we had to turn it into "drag queen"—which is still funny, in a different way.

GAIL PARENT: Blanche gives such bad dating advice in this episode, despite all her experience with men. Remember, it's not like, other than with George, she's had any really stable relationships lately that she actually would know what she's talking about. I thought it was funny, too, that Sophia ended up in bed with Cesar Romero at the end of their date—she obviously had a little nightgown tucked into that little purse she carried.

JIM VALLELY: Cesar Romero was great as Sophia's boyfriend—he brought real acting. One of my favorite things about *The Golden Girls* was getting to work with the movie greats from that age group, old pros who knew what they were doing. Don Ameche, and Howard Duff. Eddie Bracken flew in on his eightieth birthday to do our show, his first sitcom appearance. Everyone stopped by, sometimes as one of the last things they did. I don't think our generation is going to have that. What current show is Paul Newman going to do a half-hour of?

BEING A FRIEND: A CONVERSATION WITH LYLE WAGGONER

WHEN I THINK about this episode I get nostalgic, because Sonny Bono was there. What an interesting man he was—businessman, entrepreneur, politician. I had known him for a long time, because he had done *Sonny & Cher* on the stage right next to where I was working on *The Carol Burnett Show*. I also guest-starred on his show a few times—I was known as "Lyle Perfect" in some of their sketches.

Both of the shows were very popular, so I guess the *Golden Girls* producers had seen Sonny and me interacting, and thought of us when they decided to do this particular episode, with Dorothy having to decide between the short guy and the tall, egotistical guy. I loved that I didn't win and Sonny did, and the surprise ending about it all being a dream.

Doing *The Golden Girls* was a different experience for me, coming from *Carol Burnett*. Both were three-camera shows in front of a live audience, but on *The Golden Girls*, they didn't like to stop and do pickups if you made a mistake. On *Carol*, if we made a mistake, we'd usually just leave it in, because the audience got such a kick out of it. And I loved working with the ladies. I knew Betty, and had worked with Rue a few times on the road, and Bea on

Maude. But I had never met Estelle, who was so cute, and so much fun. It was such a happy set, with them all putting each other on and making each other laugh. After all, they all had such great comedy instincts.

Season 6, Episode #140: "Ebbtide's Revenge"

WRITTEN BY: Marc Sotkin
DIRECTED BY: Matthew Diamond
ORIGINAL AIR DATE: December 15, 1990
SYNOPSIS: Dorothy prepares to give the eulogy for her cross-dressing brother Phil, who has died suddenly while trying on designer knockoffs at "Big Girls Pay Less." Meanwhile, Sophia is intent on continuing her twenty-six-year feud with Phil's wife Angela (Brenda Vaccaro), who is coming to Miami for the funeral. With neither of them able to understand the reason for Sophia's anger, Dorothy convinces Angela to stay for a few days, to try to mend fences with her mother-in-law. But Sophia isn't budging; she insists on staying mad at Angela, as she claims, over a bounced dowry check. Furious at the thought that Sophia had become distant with her and Phil over a forty-seven-dollar dispute, Angela offers to write a check to make amends. But surprisingly, it is naïve Rose who recognizes what is truly going on here: Sophia is mad at Angela because she never stopped Phil

from dressing as a woman. Every time she saw her son, Sophia admits, she wondered what she had done wrong. When everyone reassures her that Phil was a good man, and that there was no shame in loving him, Sophia finally lets her true feelings show. In one of the show's few downbeat ending lines, Sophia finally mourns as she cries out, "My little boy is dead."

COMMENTARY: You may recognize guest star Brenda Vaccaro from her role in the 1984 film *Supergirl*, or from her well-known series of commercials for Playtex tampons that ran throughout the 1980s. She received a 1991 Emmy nomination for Outstanding Guest Performer in a Comedy Series for her work in this touching episode.

MARC SOTKIN: By the time of this episode, I thought we had pretty much used up the unseen character Phil comedically. He had served his purpose, and I was sort of tired of the cross-dressing jokes. What I found more interesting was, if this guy is indeed a cross-dresser, how did that happen? Everybody can make jokes about having a cross-dresser in the family, but I'll bet it messes up the dynamic in some way. His wife obviously had found some way to live with it, and to love him and raise a family with him, and I wanted to explore how she did that.

Earlier, I had written "Ebbtide," the episode where Blanche's father Big Daddy passes away, and I just didn't think I had hit the nail on the head. So I wanted another chance to look at death in the family. One of the pleasures of writing a show like *The Golden Girls* was you can write about that stuff and be both emotional and comedic. But emotionally it turned out to be a tough week. We were talking about someone's son dying, and actors don't just turn the emotions off just because they're done rehearsing. It was particularly hard for Estelle. On that Tuesday night, she actually called me and said she didn't want to do the episode. It took quite a while on the phone before I realized what was bothering her: early in the week, when we rehearsed them going to the church, Sophia originally went up to Phil's casket. But Estelle really had a problem with looking at her dead son and making jokes. It didn't feel honest to her—and she was absolutely right. So we changed it, and it became a better piece, and got nominated for a Writers' Guild Award. And I finally felt like I hit the nail on the head with this episode. It's a good thing, too, or people would have had to keep dying.

Season 6, Episode #142: "Sisters of the Bride"

WRITTEN BY: Marc Cherry & Jamie Wooten

DIRECTED BY: Matthew Diamond

ORIGINAL AIR DATE: January 12, 1991

SYNOPSIS: Blanche's brother Clayton (Monte Markham) arrives from Atlanta with a big surprise: his fiancé, Doug. Although Blanche claims to have accepted her brother's sexual orientation, seeing him with his male lover takes her aback. When Clay overhears her obsessing about what people might say, he assures her that his and Doug's commitment to each other is all that matters, and reveals that to celebrate, they plan to marry. The other ladies invite the men to the Volunteer Vanguard Awards banquet that they are producing, but in Blanche's eyes the event becomes their "coming out" party. She attends anyway, in support of her friends, but annoyingly tries to interrupt Clay from introducing his fiancé around. When it becomes obvious that Blanche has yet to truly accept her brother's alternative-lifestyle family, Clay gives her an ultimatum: come to terms with it, or stay out of it. Ultimately, wise Sophia counsels Blanche that everyone wants someone to be with as they grow older, with Clayton being no exception. When Doug assures her that he loves Clay very much, Blanche finally welcomes her future brother-in-law to the family.

COMMENTARY: Like the earlier episode "Valentine's Day," "Sisters of the Bride" matter-of-factly presents a gay marriage almost fourteen years before it became the 2004 election's hot-button issue. While this episode treads some of the same ground as did Clayton's first episode, "Scared Straight," the reappearance of the character ups the ante for Blanche, illustrating how complex the act of "acceptance" can be. Blanche ended that first episode by accepting the fact that her brother was different, but old habits and fears resurface when now she is presented with an actual, flesh-and-blood man who sleeps with her brother.

MARC SOTKIN: When Marc Cherry and Jamie Wooten first came in to pitch freelance stories to us, every show they pitched ended with "…and he's gay." Blanche meets a man and falls in love with him "… and he's gay." Dorothy's old teacher comes to visit

"… and he's gay." Every time. But when they started working full-time on staff, they were so funny and always came up with good stories. They proved they actually could come up with other concepts. So this ended up being the first gay-themed show that they did get the okay to write. After all, they were good at coming up with gay stories, and if you can't do them on *The Golden Girls* then you can't do them. So we did. And there was nothing controversial or different about that week. It was a funny script and a funny show, which made for a good week on the set.

MARC CHERRY: I never thought of this episode in the context of whether it was groundbreaking or not, maybe because I am gay and I knew all the gay storylines the show had done before as well. This was the second time Clayton was on the show, and there had been the lesbian episode as well. So for *The Golden Girls*, this was well-trod territory. We had worked together with Mitch Hurwitz to come up with the idea because it was just an easy, funny area to mine with a gay relative. This episode had just two sentences which could be seen as political, and the line is mine when Sophia says something like, "Everyone just wants someone to grow old with. Doesn't Clayton deserve that, too?" To me, that was as thought-provoking as I wanted to go, and as much as the episode needed.

We were so happy to write something with a gay character, because at the time it was still pretty rare to write gay stuff on TV. After it aired, a magnificent thing happened. We got a call from a gay couple who had gotten married who said the episode's jokes had made them smile. We went to their home, and they showed us a photo album of their wedding. It was a very sweet thing, and we found out after that that one of the men was HIV-positive. It was only about three or four years later that he passed away. I like to remember all the joy that the episode brought to them, because now they had something to relate to, like so many straight couples can when they watch TV. At the end of the episode, when Blanche hugged both her brother and his lover, it was a small but hugely important moment. It really stated something at a time when people didn't get to state that kind of stuff.

And then there was the other reaction. One Saturday, after the episode had aired, I asked Jamie to come to my apartment and wait for furniture I was having delivered. Our agents had warned us that once we became writers we should get unlisted phone numbers because the kooks will start calling, and Jamie did—but I didn't. And so when Jamie was at my apartment, he got a call from someone who started spewing the most vile stuff about how all fags are going to hell. And that we are going to hell because we wrote this episode. To me, the joke was that they called my number, and here poor Jamie was only there to do a favor for me. When it came to be five o'clock and the furniture hadn't arrived, Jamie went home because he was so shattered by this hateful person. (And of course, I later learned the furniture arrived at 5:15.)

We also found out later that Witt-Thomas received some hate mail. They're the people who put *Soap*'s gay character on the air, and so they knew enough just to ignore it. It hit Jamie and me very personally. But it also instilled in us a sense of importance, and a realization that any time you put something about gay stuff on TV, it has meaning, and it obviously hits people right in the face. Indeed, on *Desperate Housewives*, after we did the first episode where Bree's teenage son Andrew kisses his boyfriend, I got some ugly letters. One was from a mother and daughter who said they always watched the show, that it was their favorite, but that if we ever put gay things on again, they're going to stop. So I immediately went into my writers' room and said, "We've got to do another gay thing with Andrew."

Don't write your stupid little letters, and don't piss me off. Because I have the power of the pen.

JAMIE WOOTEN: We were really proud of this episode. And what it brought us was our first exposure to hate mail. The show used to get tons of letters and fan mail, and they would bring some of the interesting ones into the writers' room. After this episode aired, I was surprised we got so much hate mail. Boy, I needed to grow up fast with that stuff—I was so naïve. I saved one letter in my scrapbook, because I wanted to remember that what you do on TV can affect people, and you never know how people are going to react.

Here's the letter:
On the front, it says "The Worst Show Faggots."

"Golden girls will never be watched in our home again. It made us truly believe in abortion. Faggots are

embarssemt [sic] to the world. What's funny about 2 males acting like <u>Queers</u>. Queers should be gassed and no one should suffer their shame. Those actors should be out of work. Loinest [sic] garbage yet. Faggots disease the world. So do you."

My favorite part of the whole postcard? The "America The Beautiful" stamp.

But to put it in perspective, we got far more letters about Bea's hair than any other topic, episode or controversy ever. In general, they hated it. And they would give us very specific ways how to fix it, which I thought was hilarious—and touching that they really cared. I don't think they ever let Bea know.

Campy Guest Star Alert:

Season 6, Episode #144: Debbie Reynolds in "There Goes the Bride"

ORIGINAL AIR DATE: February 2, 1991

WHEN IT LOOKS like Dorothy is about to remarry Stan, the Girls bring in new roommate Trudy Steele, played by Debbie Reynolds. Which presents the gay viewer with a problem: we don't want Dorothy to leave, but we've loved Debbie ever since her roles in musicals like *Singin' in the Rain*, and her modern gay-friendly parts in *In & Out* and *Will & Grace*. Aw, c'mon—why can't Princess Leia's mom stay a while?

BEING A FRIEND: A CONVERSATION WITH DENA DIETRICH

I HAD WORKED with Danny Thomas on a show, *The Practice*, in the 1970s, about a doctor. So in the first season when *The Golden Girls* was casting for Dorothy's sister, Tony Thomas brought me in to audition—but I didn't get it. Then, years went by, and they wanted to bring the character, Gloria, back again. I guess they looked at me then and said well, she is tall and looks like Bea. I had even done the same part of Lucy Brown, which Bea had originated in *Threepenny Opera*.

It's interesting when you walk on any set where people have been together for a long time, because there is a closeness that the cast will have. And if you're someone new, you don't want to rush right in. So just like I did when I had played the bar owner Phil's wife Phyllis on *Murphy Brown*, I pulled back at first. I sat there and didn't say a word for the entire first day, because I was a little nervous to be in that kind of company. But everyone was wonderful to me. I had known Estelle from New York, so she and I huddled together a lot off in the corner and joked.

When I first got the part, I didn't know that Stan and Gloria wound up in bed together— then I read the whole script and I just thought it was hysterical. And I said to Herb Edelman, "Here we are again"—because strangely enough, we had played husband and wife several times. He was a wonderful man, and very easy to work with. And all the ladies just adored him. And to work with Bea was so much fun. She has such good timing, and I have good timing, and it made that whole first scene we have work really well. When I got some laughs in that scene, I thought, "Whew, I can relax—I'm okay."

Practically every week, someone comes up to me and quotes a line from the episode. Inevitably, it's a particular one of Estelle's lines, which seems to be the one people love the most. "There's a hurricane a'comin'!" Everyone expects me to know all the lines from the episode. Of course, now that I've heard that one five thousand times, I do. It blows me away when I hear from a fan about *The Golden Girls* or Mother Nature. Even though the ads went off the air long ago, Nick-at-Nite showed them for years, so people would write to me about those, too. That may trail off because I think they've stopped airing. But God knows, *The Golden Girls* will go on forever.

Campy Guest Star Alert:

Season 6, Episode #148: Alan Rachins in "Even Grandmas Get the Blues"

ORIGINAL AIR DATE: March 2, 1991

ALAN RACHINS may be playing another showbiz character here, but you'll be disappointed his Jason Stillman is no Tony Moss, Rachins's unforgettable character from the 1995 camp classic film *Showgirls*. It must be weird, not having anybody say, "I'm erect—why aren't you erect?!"

Campy Guest Star Alert:

Season 6, Episode #149: Kristy McNichol, lesbian icon, and Barney Martin in "Witness"

ORIGINAL AIR DATE: March 9, 1991

IN THIS EPISODE, Kristy McNichol, a lesbian favorite, appears as Barbara Weston, her character from *Golden Girls* spinoff *Empty Nest*. Two later *Girls* episodes also feature Dinah Manoff—Marti from the movie *Grease*—playing her *Nest* role of Barbara's sister Carol. And playing Rose's new boyfriend, aka Mafia killer "The Cheeseman," is Barney Martin, the actor who originated the role of "Mr. Cellophane" in the 1975 Broadway production of *Chicago,* before becoming better known as Jerry's father on *Seinfeld*.

Campy Guest Star Alert:

Season 6, Episode #153: George Hearn in "Henny Penny—Straight, No Chaser"

ORIGINAL AIR DATE: May 4, 1991

WHEN THE GIRLS become last-minute replacements for sick schoolkids in a musical production of *Henny Penny*, Theater Queens take notice: Foxy Loxy's meat-eating grin might look familiar—and so might all the feathery costumes. Actor George Hearn played the butchering barber *Sweeney Todd* on Broadway in 1979–80, and originated the character of Armand in the original 1983 production of *La Cage Aux Folles*.

Campy Guest Star Alert:

Season 7, Episode #156: Edie McClurg as Nurse DeFarge in "Beauty and the Beast"

ORIGINAL AIR DATE: October 5, 1991

SHE WAS *The Hogan Family*'s perky neighbor Mrs. Poole, and *Ferris Bueller*'s school secretary. Now, Edie McClurg turns up for a fun guest spot as imposing Nurse DeFarge—named for the villainous knitter in Charles Dickens's *A Tale of Two Cities*. Although scary to Sophia at first, she soon muscles in on the other Girls' turf, upsetting especially Dorothy as she gains permission to call her patient "Ma."

Campy Guest Star Alert:

Season 7, Episode #161: Dena Dietrich as Gloria Petrillo in "The Monkey Show"

ORIGINAL AIR DATE: November 9, 1991

DOROTHY SHOULD BE relieved when her yutz of an ex-husband tells her he's over her, and moving on with his life. But unfortunately, it's her sister Gloria he's moving on with. When Dorothy catches them in bed together, the ensuing storm of sibling rivalry is matched only by the giant hurricane brewing outside.

This two-part episode comprised one hour's worth of a hurricane theme night that blew through all three of NBC's Saturday night sitcoms—the others being fellow Witt-Thomas productions *Empty Nest* and *Nurses*. Since all three shows were set in Miami, NBC's Warren Littlefield had requested a "November sweeps" stunt where characters could cross over from show to show. So, that night, *Nest*'s Dinah Manoff checked in on the *Girls*, while Sophia visited *Nest* neighbors the Westons and Rose showed up at *Nurses'* Community Medical Center. The stunt worked; the high winds produced monster ratings.

Ironically, although Gloria is now house-bound in Miami due to bad weather, actress Dena Dietrich is best known to many fans as "Mother Nature" from the popular series of TV ads for Chiffon margarine that ran from 1971–79. Is it just a coincidence that first Gloria gets confronted by her sister, and now there's a hurricane a'comin?

Beware, Dorothy—haven't you heard it's not nice to fool [with] Mother Nature?

Campy Guest Star Alert:

Season 7, Episode #164: Phil Leeds in "Ro$e Love$ Mile$"

ORIGINAL AIR DATE: November 16, 1991

HERE PLAYING Guido Spirelli, Sophia's spurned first suitor, the prolific character actor Phil Leeds had a recurring role at the time of his 1998 death on *Everybody Loves Raymond*, where he played Ray's ancient uncle who was obsessed with people knowing he and his roommate weren't gay lovers.

Campy Guest Star Alert:

Season 7, Episode #167: Steven Gilborn in "The Pope's Ring"

ORIGINAL AIR DATE: December 14, 1991

IF THE PRIEST who comes to the house looks familiar, it's because the actor, Steven Gilborn, went on to play quite a different kind of father—*Ellen*'s PFLAG-waving pop.

BEING A FRIEND: A CONVERSATION WITH BETTY GARRETT

ALMOST EVERY actor wanted to be on *The Golden Girls*, and I was very happy with the part of Sarah, because the story line was very sweet and was a departure for me on TV. I had the reputation of being a comedian, and I liked the fact that this story was quite serious and dramatic. In fact, I don't remember having any jokes, and I really didn't mind. I had one long monologue, and I'll always be grateful to Bea for what she said to me. In between shots, she looked at me and said, "You're such a good actress." I just treasured that. Because I had done a lot of serious parts, but when you get the reputation of just being a funny girl, you don't get that compliment often.

Campy Guest Star Alert

Season 7, Episode #168: Betty Garrett in "Old Boyfriends"

ORIGINAL AIR DATE: January 4, 1991

SOPHIA SHOPS for a man in a senior citizens' personals column and meets Marvin (Louis Guss), who seems great. The problem is, supposedly because his eyesight is too poor for him to drive, the lovebirds are escorted everywhere by Marvin's sister, Sarah (Betty Garrett). When Sophia tries to get Marvin alone, the touching truth comes out: Sarah is actually Marvin's dying wife, and is trying to find a replacement who will care for him after she goes. It's a beautiful story, but the truly fun part is the casting—guest star Betty Garrett is an accomplished film and stage actress and a TV legend, having played both landlady Mrs. Edna Babish on *Laverne & Shirley* and recurring neighbor Irene Lorenzo on *All in the Family*.

Season 7, Episode #169: "Goodbye, Mr. Gordon"

WRITTEN BY: Gail Parent & Jim Vallely

DIRECTED BY: Lex Passaris

ORIGINAL AIR DATE: January 11, 1992

SYNOPSIS: Dorothy is giddy as a schoolgirl when her eleventh grade teacher Mr. Gordon (James Callahan) visits. Sophia remembers the huge crush Dorothy had on him, recalling how she used to help him grade papers, do his laundry and even rotate his tires. Once he arrives, Dorothy turns into a giggly seventeen-year-old all over again. During lunch, Mr. Gordon talks about an article he's writing and how he can't get his thoughts organized, and Dorothy enthusiastically volunteers to help.

Meanwhile, Rose has been promoted to associate producer of the *Wake Up, Miami* show and is looking for two women to join the panel discussion she has created on "Women Who Live Together." Blanche jumps at the chance for TV exposure, and volunteers, as does Dorothy. On the day of the taping, Mr. Gordon shows up at the studio and showers Dorothy with flowers and a good luck kiss. Dorothy is shocked—but not as shocked as she becomes once the cameras roll. "Women Who Live Together" is about lesbians!

After several days of being mad at Rose, Blanche eventually forgives her, even though now the only people asking her out are women. In the meantime, Dorothy invests days' worth of work on Mr. Gordon's article—only to have him turn around and publish it under his own name. Disillusioned and hurt, Dorothy tells him off and asks him to leave. She complains to her mother that her teenage fantasy of Mr. Gordon as a Sir Lancelot coming to her rescue is now tarnished. Sophia reminds her that she gives too much, and in the end gets hurt. "But keeping fantasies alive is a part of life."

COMMENTARY: It's a question, often whispered, that many of us have at some time dreaded hearing spoken: "They're single, over thirty, and they live together? Are they gay?" These days, it's something one wonders about any longtime, same-sex roommates. And with this episode, it's a question *The Golden Girls* gets to enjoy cleverly playing with as well.

JIM VALLELY: We had fun writing a lot of the jokes in this episode, like the questions that Sophia stands up and asks to embarrass Blanche and Dorothy while in the audience at *Wake Up, Miami.* I also remember having a big fight with one of our producers, Nina Wass, about this one. I had begged her please, please when the camera cuts to Dorothy on the talk show, please put a chyron underneath the shot that says, "Dorothy, a Lesbian." Nina promised she would, but then somewhere along the way, someone didn't. I never knew why.

Season 7, Episode #173: "Journey to the Center of Attention"

WRITTEN BY: Marc Cherry & Jamie Wooten
DIRECTED BY: Lex Passaris
ORIGINAL AIR DATE: February 22, 1992
SYNOPSIS: Blanche coerces a lonely Dorothy into joining her for a night of excitement at her favorite bar hangout. Once there, Blanche is soon dethroned as the queen of the Rusty Anchor when the patrons take an instant liking to Dorothy, whose singing makes her the new center of attention. To regain her stature, Blanche plans to beat Dorothy at her own game, with a sexy number sung atop the bar's piano. But her rendition of "I Wanna Be Loved By You" goes clumsily and hilariously wrong, sending Blanche running in tears for the ladies' room. Dorothy runs after her, and the two Girls admit to times when they are jealous of each other. And although neither is willing to give up her night of adoration at the Rusty Anchor, they come to an amicable settlement: they'll split up the nights of the week.
COMMENTARY: *The Golden Girls* had found a few earlier excuses to get Bea Arthur singing: she belted "Miami,

You've Got Style" as the Girls entered a songwriting contest, impersonated Cher on "I've Got You, Babe," and added a *basso profundo* "Yessss?" to the Girls' crib-side lullaby of "Mr. Sandman." But this episode gives us Bea performing two classic tunes, "Hard-Hearted Hannah" and "What'll I Do," leaving the patrons of the Rusty Anchor—undoubtedly the gayest dockside straight bar in all of Miami—calling out for an encore.

And "Journey to the Center of Attention" provides a second treat with Rue's musical number, as she attempts to writhe sexily on the bar's piano like an older Michelle Pfeiffer in *The Fabulous Baker Boys*. But unlike Michelle, when Blanche kicks up her heel, she loses a shoe. When she plays with the microphone cord, she nearly strangles a customer. And when she slides up to the pianist, she falls right on her eighty-eights. It's one of the series' best bits of physical comedy.

BEA ARTHUR: This was such a funny episode, and Rue was so wonderful in it. I loved that it showed both Dorothy and Blanche to be so real, having real jealousies.

RUE MCCLANAHAN: I like doing physical comedy, and I like to sing. And I knew that the bit on the piano would have to be choreographed precisely for it to look that sloppy and in the moment. I had recently co-written the book for a musical farce at the Golden Theater in Burbank called *Oedipus Shmoedipus, As Long As You Loved Your Mother*, set in 457 B.C. Athens, and had worked with a choreographer named Gregory Scott

Young. So I asked him to come in to *The Golden Girls* and help me work out Blanche's moves for that scene. I told him I wanted Blanche to just make a shambles of the song, and he came up with some very funny stuff, like the shoe flying off. We did it by the numbers, and I learned it meticulously. And then I had to do it like it was happening spontaneously and surprising Blanche. I was so relieved when I got through it without mishap and had to do it only once at each taping of the show. But I can't think of anything I enjoyed doing more as Blanche.

Sharing Cheesecake with Bea Arthur

Q QUOTE: "I hate cheesecake. I didn't like the cheesecake scenes, either—I didn't find them amusing, and thought of them as just a segue. But audiences love it, and to this day they still talk about it. And when I do my one-woman show and talk about this, people will come backstage and say, "Do you really love cheesecake? Don't lie!"

THE FIRST THING I noticed about *The Golden Girls* pilot was that it was a beautiful script. It had an extra character, a gay houseman, who was very charming, but they cut him by the very next episode. I don't think they had any idea that just the four of us would be so strong together. And we were lucky enough to have brilliant writers on the show and a fabulous director, Terry Hughes. It was a great combination of all the elements.

I think the relationship between Dorothy and her mother makes for one of the most brilliant comedic duos I've ever known. First of all it was so ludicrous, with the fact that physically Estelle and I are so completely different. And then their love/hate relationship, where they could be so sweet yet so cutting with each other, was so real, and was just marvelous the way it was written. I also loved Dorothy's relationship with Stan. She could be so mad at him, and claim she hated him, but the lines were written to say that they obviously still loved each other. And so it became a comedic relationship that really paid off.

I remember one scene where Stan is staying over, and I've made him sleep on the floor. The camera is on me, and suddenly I hear him laughing. And I have a line like, "Stanley, if you're doing what I think you're doing …" I remember saying to the writer, "How are we permitted to do this?" We certainly got away from the censors more than we had on *Maude*, where every third day of every week we had to read the entire script to the network and then Norman Lear would start his negotiations with them. "I'll cut that line or that section, but Bea has to say that line." It was one fight after another. And that struck me when we were doing "Journey to the Center of Attention" in the seventh season, and Rue does a thing where she sits in a guy's lap and does the "is that a gun or are you just happy to see me" joke. But it seems like that leeway came with time, because in the pilot episode, we had to change the line where Sophia calls Blanche's fiancé a "douchebag."

Sometimes rather than a written line, the

writers would want a reaction shot from one of us. They and Terry were so good at knowing what was and was not going to work. People always ask me about my "slow burn." I just know that I tried to keep my reactions honest. I didn't even start out doing comedy, but I think you have to be real. So many really brilliant actors, once they are told that they're in a comedy, turn into people from another planet. There is no similarity between their characters and reality. So you just have to make sure as an actor to make everything real for yourself.

That had been easier on *Maude*, because we taped on Tuesdays, which meant we had a few days over the weekend of not rehearsing where suddenly it would pop into my head "I know how to do that!" But there were at least a few things about Dorothy that were easy for me to find real, because they are like me. I always tell people we're both five feet nine and a half inches in our stocking feet, and both of us have very deep voices. But we're also the same in that like Dorothy, I hate bullshit. I call it bubble-pricking. Being the great leveler, the voice of reason who brings other people back down to earth. Dorothy was the voice of reason on that show. Left to their own devices, I don't know how the other women could have survived.

People often ask me how I didn't break up, with all the outrageous things all the Girls did and said. But there was one show where I just broke up and broke up and broke up. It was an episode where there was a charity auction, and Don Johnson was supposed to emcee. This was at the height of *Miami Vice*'s popularity—all the men were doing the no-socks thing. But at the last minute, they announced on stage that Don couldn't make it, but he had sent his wardrobe. And they held up a hanger with a white jacket on it—I've never seen anything funnier in my life. I couldn't not break up. I think eventually they had to just cut away from me. And if I saw it again today, I'm sure I would react the same way.

I also get asked all the time if we're going to do a reunion. But the way I see it, why would we? We're not going to be any better than we were, or top some of the great shows we did. I left *Maude* after six years and *Golden Girls* after seven, because even then, I realized we couldn't top what we'd already done. *Golden Girls* started to strain a bit by the end, and wasn't as hysterical as it had been, so I thought it was time to leave. Today, I still have people constantly recognizing me, saying, "Oh my God, it's Dorothy!" It is so sweet and so nice. Often, flight attendants will come up and say something to me when I'm traveling. After all these years, I am delighted. It is incredible when you realize, *The Golden Girls* is all over the globe.

CELEBRITY SURVEY #4:

WHAT IS YOUR FAVORITE *GIRLS* EPISODE?

THE ONE WHERE the Girls are dragged off to jail as prostitutes. The only thing funnier than Rose behind bars is Dorothy in the same predicament.

—Ben Patrick Johnson,
author of *Third and Heaven*

THE ONE WHERE Ruby Dee comes to get the music box back from Blanche that she'd gifted to Blanche's father.

—Doug Spearman, actor

THE ONE WHERE Blanche's brother comes out of the closet. Because it said it's time to open up a dialogue about this and stop living in the shadows. These four women are not of the generation that you'd think would be accepting about gay issues. But here it is square in their face, and they handled it beautifully.

—ANT, stand-up comedian and
host of VH1's *Celebrity Fit Club*

THE ONE WHERE Blanche's baby brother turned out to be gay. Generally speaking, I liked the shows that dealt with real issues. One of my favorite things about the show was how we held on their stunned reactions right before breaking for a commercial as the music kicks in. Very Mexican Soap Opera.

—Craig Chester, actor/writer/director
of *Adam & Steve*

THE ONE WHERE Rose tries to learn to skydive to spice up her relationship with Miles. It reminded me of the compromising I do to keep my relationships with so many. Wait a minute—Is this therapy?

—Jermaine Taylor, panelist,
GSN's *I've Got a Secret*

THE ONE WHERE there's a drought in St. Olaf, so Rose isn't allowed to have sex until it rains.

—Bruce Daniels, comic

THE CHRISTMAS EPISODE where they get stuck in a diner away from their families. Some of the best holidays happen with just your friends.

—Dan Mathews, vice president of People for
the Ethical Treatment of Animals (PETA)

THE ONE WHERE Rose tells mean old Frieda Claxton to drop dead and she does! I love when people follow orders.

—Frank DeCaro, talk show host,
Sirius Satellite Radio and panelist
on GSN's *I've Got a Secret*

THE ONE WHERE Rose wishes dead the old lady who wants the tree torn down. It shows another side of Rose's personality, that maybe she is a little more savvy than they usually give her credit for.

–Derek Hartley, talk show host,
Sirius Satellite Radio

THE ONE WHERE Dorothy tries to surprise her mother by bringing her aunt over from Sicily—and who should show up but Nancy Walker. It was like the battle of the mini-mamas, and to me there's nothing funnier than watching short ladies insulting each other. It should be an Olympic category.

–Jaffe Cohen, stand-up comedian
and author of the novel *Tush*

THE ONE WHERE Dorothy almost marries Stan for the second time. But then Stan shows his true colors and Dorothy's smarts kick in. When I think how many times that has happened to me with just friends...OY!

—Mark Lund, television personality

THE ONE WHERE Dorothy's cross-dressing brother Phil dies. The scene at the end with Sophia acknowledging that her youngest child has passed on is just heart-wrenching. And also the one where Rose thinks she kills men by sleeping with them. Her monologue where she tells the Girls that she's killed Arnie and the local sheriff through sex is Betty White at her best.

–Dennis Hensley, "Twist" radio host and author of Misadventures in the (213)

THE ONE WHERE Dorothy's lesbian friend develops feelings for Rose. It was the mid-80s and anything gay on TV was all about us dying of AIDS, but this was so funny and the character said such beautiful things.

–Suzanne Westenhoefer, stand-up comedian and panelist, GSN's I've Got a Secret

THE ONE WHERE Blanche and Sophia are fighting over the same man, Fidel.

–Zulema Griffin, fashion designer

THE LAST EPISODE, where Dorothy is marrying Leslie Nielsen, and we hear her thoughts out loud—and so does he.

–Bruce Vilanch, writer/performer

WHAT IS *YOUR* FAVORITE *GIRLS* EPISODE?

The Girls Are Still Golden Today

"During the production of only the third or fourth episode, I was watching a run-through with Paul Witt. I remember turning and saying to him that what these amazing women are doing is going to be like [Lucy]. He looked at me as if to say, 'We'll see,' and I could have been wrong. But I've sat through a lot of run-throughs, and I've never had the same feeling that the material was clearly so universal and timeless, we'll still be laughing at it thirty, forty, fifty years later."

—Tony Thomas

PICTURE IT: New York City. On a midweek afternoon, hundreds of fans crowd inside a Barnes & Noble bookstore, and hundreds more huddle outside in the rain—all hoping for a moment with three of their idols. Finally, more than six hours after the line was officially established, there they are. At first glimpse, the crowd calls out passionately for them, as if they are about to take the stage and burn up their electric guitars. But no, these three women are slightly older than your typical rock stars (even Mick Jagger and Tina Turner). Two are octogenarians and one is younger—in her seventies, that is. And—

All right, fine. By this time, you know those three women are none other than *The Golden Girls* themselves, Bea Arthur, Betty White, and Rue McClanahan. And you're probably also not surprised that these women have the power to elicit such strong reaction from their fans. That November 22, 2005, as a crowd heavy on young girls and gay men filled the Barnes & Noble in Manhattan's gay Chelsea neighborhood, the store quickly sold out of the show's third season DVD sets.

A few of those at the front of the line had earned their spots by camping out overnight on the sidewalk, or, like a girl named Lindsay, by driving all night from Boston with her mother and sister. Two NYU students named Nya and Erin passed the time by leading fellow fans in a sing-along of "Thank You for Being a Friend." Then, more than an hour before the Girls' allotted signing time was to begin, bookstore employees had to cut off the queue at five hundred people. And so more fans took to the rainy street, piling five and six deep in front of the store's north- and east-facing windows. There, as the three-hours-long signing commenced, one young male fan scored the moment he was hoping for: Betty saw his homemade sign pressed up against the pane, "I'M SERIOUS—WILL YOU SHARE CHEESECAKE WITH ME?!" She made a pantomime motion for being way too full, and the two of them shared a laugh, six feet and several inches of glass apart.

By the summer of 2006—fourteen years after *The Golden Girls* ended its original run—the show was still drawing eleven million viewers per week and thirty million per month on the Lifetime cable network, its home since 1997. Although up against much newer sitcom competition, any given one of the show's seven daily airings still ranked among the top three "off-network" sitcoms shown by Lifetime, and among the top seven on any cable channel.

"There aren't too many shows from 1985 which hold up like that," notes Tim Brooks, Lifetime's Vice President of Research and the co-author with Earle Marsh of the TV fan's bible, *The Complete Directory to Prime Time Network and Cable TV Shows: 1946-*

Present. Tim explains that the steady viewership of *The Golden Girls* and its spinoff *Golden Palace*, barely changed since 1997, is very unusual. After all, over the course of those nine years, most of us viewers have aged into the next Nielsen age group—and some viewers, unfortunately, just plain die off. Yet, for example, the dinnertime airings of *The Golden Girls*, at 6:00 and 6:30 p.m., attracted 1.1 million viewers back in 1999, and still drew 1.1 million by 2005. So obviously, the show must be continually attracting new fans to replace those who, for one reason or another, leave. "That's unusual because with all the competition out there, shows of any kind usually tend to wear out," Tim says. "But *The Golden Girls* has turned out to be a long-distance runner."

The show has also turned out to be a boon for Lifetime in that it attracts a wider audience than the network's typical fare. As Tim explains, whereas the typical Lifetime Original Movie tends to attract women in mostly the middle age ranges, the *Girls's* appeal is not age-specific. Younger women, older women—*The Golden Girls* is one of the few shows they all share. And since the network in general pulls strong ratings among African-American women, so does *The Golden Girls*. As Tim explains, "The show has a lot of gender appeal rather than being based on race or age."

And although the AC Nielsen Company does not yet measure their viewership as its own demographic, everyone knows anecdotally that *The Girls* mean an awful lot to The Gays (as does Lifetime itself). As marketers continue to get hip to gays' fabled disposable income, a few smaller research companies are beginning to track trends in gay viewership. And in the test data they have produced, Tim says, *The Golden Girls* does very well among gays; it's a top-ten cable show.

The Golden Girls of the O.C.

IN ANOTHER sure sign that *The Golden Girls* has spawned a new generation of fans, the ladies of the eighties have earned multiple shout-outs on the hip, new-millennium teen soap *The O.C.* In a first season episode of the Fox network hit entitled "The Third Wheel," romantic rivals Summer (Rachel Bilson) and Anna (Samaire Armstrong) bonded as they sang "Thank You for Being a Friend" in front of the ladies' room mirror at a rock concert, revealing their mutual love for all things *Golden*.

Why did these two girls from Orange County turn out to be fans of the *Girls* of Dade County? Series creator Josh Schwartz admits that he got the idea to turn Summer into a Blanche fan by eavesdropping on one of Rachel Bilson's real-life conversations. When he heard that Rachel—a devout viewer of the show's repeats on Lifetime—and three of her friends watched *The Golden Girls* together, each identifying with a different character, he decided to write their devotion into his own show. "I had no idea the show was so big among younger people," Josh admits. "But I figured Rachel and her friends are pretty hip ladies. If they watched it …"

Josh says that he himself grew up watching the *Girls*, "although it makes no sense. I was ten years old—what could I possibly relate to about four senior citizens in

Florida? But yet, I tuned in every week." Two decades later, Josh had that very sentiment come out of his heroine Summer's mouth.

"Their *Golden Girls* moment was the bridge to their friendship," Josh explains. More than two years later, Anna unexpectedly returned to Newport Beach in the April 2006 episode "The Party Favor," and reassured Summer, "You're still my Blanche, you know." And so, what was intended as a one-time reference has grown into an extended, multi-year metaphor for female friendship. Josh says that the fans love it—"It's amazing how many people in their twenties we've heard from, who really connected with *The Golden Girls* scenes." And that includes one of his leading ladies. "Rachel was thrilled," he adds. "But she was also a little wary of ever speaking in front of me again."

Golden Girls: The Next Generation

Q QUOTE: "Right from the beginning, young people liked the show. I thought and thought about why and I finally realized, it is because the show may have been about older ladies, but it was still very anti-establishment."

–*Bea Arthur*

NIELSEN ALSO does not compile any specific ratings tracking viewership by college students, but Lifetime knows from their feedback that they are yet another niche audience, watching in huge numbers. Tim Brooks says that of the 250 to 300 emails the network receives per month about the show, about 30 percent are from people in college or college-age. And Betty White corroborates that pattern, explaining that to this day, 70 percent of the mail she receives about *The Golden Girls* is from fans under age 25.

A young-skewing audience like that might be expected for repeats of a more recent show like *Friends*—but today's college students were most likely not yet born when *The Golden Girls* premiered in 1985. So why would people in their teens and twenties have discovered and developed such a devotion to broads who even back then were old enough to be their grandmothers? "Ever since Tony Bennett showed up on MTV's *Unplugged*, old has become cool," Tim theorizes. "As long as the old people are cool in their demeanor and share the same values and beliefs, they can be fun people to be around." Tim adds that unlike previous generations which rebelled against anything reminiscent of their elders, today's younger set can see past the age of *The Golden Girls* because they relate to their liberated lifestyle and the love they show to their non-traditional, non-nuclear family. "It's like having a really cool aunt."

The Golden Girls has become one of the rare shows to develop this whole new generation of fans—a critical achievement, because nostalgia can only carry a show so far. After all, older fans eventually die off or just move on to something else—hence the reason, Tim says, why today we don't see too many repeats, aside from *I Love Lucy*, of anything from the 1950s. Ultimately, he explains, the shows that stick around are the ones, from any era, that continue to touch and tickle new people—and that's why he predicts that the *Girls* will still be popular twenty years from now, just like *Lucy*. "Shows that remain very popular are not specific to their times—they're just well written, about funny people. These are happy comedies for the middle of the night when you want to go to bed with your head clear. Like *The Golden Girls*, they're easy-to-watch television."

ACKNOWLEDGMENTS

Janine Damura, for her expert and invaluable assistance

Frank DeCaro, without whose continued love and support this book would not be possible

Susan Harris, Paul Junger Witt and Tony Thomas, for creating a show that has inspired lives, never mind this book

Joe Pittman and the staff at Alyson Books, for their vision, guidance, and patience

My interviewees: Kevin Abbott, Garth Ancier, Bea Arthur, Susan Beavers, Doris Belack, James Berg, Raye Birk, John Bowab, Randy Brenner, Paul Chapdelaine, Marc Cherry, Jo DeWinter, Matthew Diamond, Dena Dietrich, Ellen Albertini Dow, Jim Drake, Ja'Net DuBois, Debra Engle, Judy Evans Steele, Tracy Gamble, Betty Garrett, Carl Gettleman, Pamela Golum, Harold Gould, Juliet Green, Lyn Greene, Susan Harris, Sandy and Harriet Helberg, Winifred Hervey, Terry Hughes, Mitchell Hurwitz, Allison Jones, Jeffrey Jones, Stephen Jones, Ken Kercheval, Charles Levin, Warren Littlefield, Christopher Lloyd, Cheech Marin, Monte Markham, Rue McClanahan, Mort Nathan, Lois Nettleton, Michael Orland, Gail Parent, Lex Passaris, Marco Pennette, Patrik-Ian Polk, Julie Poll, Peggy Pope, Paul Provenza, Alan Rachins, Doris Roberts, Jay Sandrich, John Schaefer & Peter Mac, Josh Schwartz, Don Seigel, Robert Spina, Maurice Stein, Lynne Marie Stewart, Elaine Stritch, Jay Thomas,

Tony Thomas, Joel Thurm, Richard Vaczy, Jim Vallely, Chick Vennera, Lyle Waggoner, Nina Wass, Richard Weaver, Betty White, Paul Junger Witt, Don Woodard, Jamie Wooten, Kent Zbornak, and Stan Zimmerman

My survey respondents: ANT, John Bartlett, Bryan Batt, Douglas Carter Beane, Tom Bianchi, Keith Boykin, Dan Bucatinsky, Ted Casablanca, Craig Chester, Jaffe Cohen, Bruce Daniels, Frank DeCaro, Tammy Etheridge, Ari Gold, Judy Gold, Zulema Griffin, Derek Hartley, Dennis Hensley, Ben Patrick Johnson, Randy Jones, Rex Lee, Mark Lund, Billy Masters, Dan Mathews, Varla Jean Merman, Bob Smith, Doug Spearman, Jermaine Taylor, Tony Tripoli, Robert Verdi, Bruce Vilanch, Suzanne Westenhoefer and Paul J. Williams

Angela Allen; Pat Altomare; Julie Bush; Fran Bascom; Ellen Benjamin; Erica Berger; Doria Biddle; Steve Bluestein; John Bowab; Robyn Burt; Carolyn Callahan; Frank Carabineris & Chuck Hettinger; David Stephen Cohen; Angelo, Mary Kate, Tom, Joe and Alison Colucci; Marty Colucci & John Volland; Allen Crowe; Carr D'Angelo & Susan Avallone; Patti D'Arbanville; Bonnie Datt & Chris Lowe; Frank DeCaro Sr.; Wendy Diamond; Lois Draegin; Donna Ellerbusch; Ramin Fathie; Marlene Fuentes; Bill Funt; Dwight Garcia; Dave Gorab; Carin Greenberg-Baker; Barbara Haigh; Glen Hanson; Steve Hasley; Karen & Eric Herman; The Academy of Television Arts and Sciences' Archive Project; Kelly Hicks; Joel Hornstock; Todd Jackson & Danielle Perez; Bonnie Johanson; Allison Jones; Hollis Jordan; Phyllis Katz; Susan Kim; Jay Kogen; Sue Kogen; Jennifer Lang; Karen, Rick, Jake and Elyssa Langberg; Barbara Lawrence; Steve

LeGrice; David Logan; Eric McCool; Cathryn Michon; Marija Mikolajczak, Amanda Bell, Alexis DiVincenti, Ann Toback, Chris Albers and the Animation and Organizing Committees of the WGA-East; Allan Neuwirth; Sharon Packer; Lex & Lulu Passaris; Dan Pasternack; Marsha Posner Williams; Larry Raab; Todd Rosentover & Alycia Weinberger; Richard Samson; Rich Sands; Andi Schechter; Susan Salkow Shapiro, Art Rutter and the Shapiro-Lichtman Agency; Jordan Sonnenblick; Sally Starin & June Ploch; Rochell Thomas; Marcia Wallace; Gene Walsh; Deborah Warren; Tom Wheeler; Morrow Wilson; Don Woodard; Andy Yerkes; Burt Dubrow, Jean Wiegman and the cast and crew of GSN's *I've Got a Secret*; the crew of *The Frank DeCaro Show* on Sirius Satellite Radio OutQ; the Knops, Skaggs, Harbaugh, Simonetty, Colucci, Vanas, Dige and Thomas families.